Praise for *Lead the Way* an

"*Lead the Way* is an inspirational guide for those of us who want to enjoy the journey of leadership!" —***Marshall Goldsmith***, *#1 New York Times Bestselling Author of Triggers, MOJO and What Got You Here Won't Get You There*

"Inside Out Leadership is simply a great book for leaders to use in their own personal development. Use the book to put yourself in your own "time out" and make space for self-reflection - the key ingredient in being accountable for your own success and happiness. Robb's sage advice helps you learn to live skillfully and joyfully in your current circumstances rather than pining for a different reality in order to be happy. So get silent, get reflective, and listen to your own call to greatness - Then go pass it on." —***Cy Wakeman***, *New York Times Bestselling Author of No Ego, Reality-Based Leadership, and Reality-Based Rules of the Workplace*

"Before you can lead others, you must know yourself. Robb Holman provides a good foundation for self-knowledge that can help you lead more effectively." —***John Baldoni***, *Inc.com Top 50 Leadership Expert, Executive Coach and Author of 13 books including MOXIE: The Secret to Bold and Gutsy Leadership*

"Robb Holman has written a foundational must-read! *Lead the Way* is a guide to leadership principles that will change the way you look at leadership. Adapted from his coaching program, *Lead the Way* will help you hone in on your life's purpose from the inside out to understand who you are and be more effective in leading those around you - in your professional, as well as personal, communities." —***Dan Rockwell***, *Inc Magazine Top 50 Leadership Expert and Author of the Leadership Freak Blog*

"Life is about meaning. But how do you get there when you're on the treadmill of seemingly nonstop work and family? Robb Holman shows us the way via intriguing and personal examples and techniques that open a window for all of us to live the productive and happy life we dream of." —***Sydney Finkelstein***, *Professor & Director of the Center for Leadership at the Tuck School of Business at Dartmouth College and Bestselling Author of SUPERBOSSES: How Exceptional Leaders Master the Flow of Talent*

"A Valuable book that will help you rise to your greatest life."—**Robin Sharma**, *worldwide bestselling author of The Leader Who Had No Title + founder of The Titan Academy*

"Focus and vision drive success. Robb's Inside Out Leadership perspective helps entrepreneurs and other leaders tap into both in profound ways." — **Justin E. Crawford**, *Bestselling Author of Live Free or DIY*

Lead the Way takes readers on a journey of self-discovery, helping them become the person they need to be in order to lead effectively. Soulful yet scientific, author Robb Holman gives leaders a framework for finally applying the popular adage, "Before you can lead others, you must learn to lead yourself."—**Ron Friedman, Ph.D.**, *author of The Best Place to Work: The Art and Science of Creating an Extraordinary Workplace*

"The Inside Out Leadership program is a catalyst for positive change that has sticking-power to drive results. If you're looking to make changes that will lead to profound differences in your life, then it has to come from the Inside Out. Robb has appropriately named his leadership program for that reason. He leads you through a powerful process of self-discovery that taps into our core passions, purpose, and vision for life." —**Steve Van Valin**, *Founder & CEO of Culturology*

"Working with Robb and his Inside Out Leadership program has had a profound impact on me as a leader. More importantly, the program has helped me grow as a person. Honesty, vulnerability, and passion are keys to connecting with a team, and Robb's approach cultivates all of these values to make me a better leader, husband, and father." —**Stephen McSherry**, *President of Penn Tank Lines*

"Robb's coaching experience and techniques were just what I needed when I was trying to expand my business. Robb introduced me to his Inside Out Leadership approach. By following his philosophy, I grew my small consulting business from one to three clients within six months, hired an assistant, and engaged with a consultant to help manage the expanding workload. For that I am very grateful!" —**Melissa J. Scrimo**, *M.A. President & Founder of Applied Intelligence Consulting*

"Inside out leadership showed me what was missing in my business. I lacked focus and direction, and after going through the Inside Out Leadership process I gained the clarity needed to take my business to the next level! Now, I am much more fulfilled, happy, and focused in what I'm doing, and the results have been amazing, both personally and professionally. Thank you Inside Out Leadership!" —*Chris LaGarde*, *Co-Founder of The Chris & Caleb Real Estate Team*

"Your personal purpose and vision are elusive ideas, untouchable, yet they must always be front and center in your mind and heart because they are intertwined with everything in your life. This is the Inside Out Leadership philosophy that Robb introduced to and instilled in me. It will last a lifetime, offering a constant core of wisdom and encouragement. Be patient. There is no magic pill for this." —*Ryan Gerardi*, *Founder & Owner, AutoConversion*

"Working with Robb's Inside Out Leadership program brought clarity and vision to a new role I was taking on at my company. It kept me focused on the big picture and broke down challenges into manageable pieces. This program not only made me a better leader at work but it has carried over to my personal life and made me a better father, husband, and coach." —*Ken Jeinnings*, *President of Lawn & Golf Supply Co, Inc.*

"Robb Holman's Inside Out Leadership philosophy gets right to the core of what makes me a unique individual. It teaches me how I can use my gifts and talents to show up in the world, every day, being the best version of myself. This philosophy allows me to give myself permission and feel empowered to unapologetically make my mark on the world." —*Beth Eldredge*, *President & Founder of Eldredge Cleaning*

"Learning to lead from the inside out from Robb Holman has enabled me to become the person and the leader God created me to be. There's no place better to be than in alignment with God's will for me. I feel more alive, more connected, more empathetic, and more empowered with the people I work with, my family and my friends. Thank you Robb Holman for teaching me how to live from the inside out!" —*Robert Lehman*, *SAP NA Analytics Business Partner*

"Robb Holman's Inside Out Leadership has helped me gain valuable insight and lessons on how to manage my own company, which has led me in the direction of working with a variety of nonprofit organizations. I get to use my management and marketing skills while knowing that I am making a difference. I have become happier and more successful...personally, professionally and financially, by adopting his Inside Out philosophy." —*Diane McGraw, Founder & President of McGraw Productions*

"Working with Robb has been an incredible experience. You quickly realize that everything is connected. In business we tend to focus on the things we can see. The reality is, everything flows from the inside out. Happiness is an inside job. A fulfilled person is more efficient, organized, and a better leader. All of these things touch every area of your business and before you know it, the unseen catches up to the seen. I would highly recommend anyone in a leadership position to read this book and connect with the author." —*Corey Curyto, Partner & COO of Maven Creative*

LEAD THE WAY

Inside Out Leadership™
Principles For Business Owners & Leaders

Robb Holman

Lulu Publishing Services rev. date: 10/16/2017

I dedicate this book to God, who has given me purpose so I can help others with theirs, my wife and my children who have inspired me beyond words, and my core LTW team for all of your work, encouragement, and support in this very important project.

CONTENTS

FOREWORD

I SAT IN A COMFORTABLE booth at P.F. Chang's reconnecting with a long-lost former colleague. Catching up was long overdue, and we blurted out war stories and things that had happened since we'd last seen each other. Suddenly, she stopped in the middle of a sentence and became animated. It was as if she just remembered having a winning lottery ticket in her purse.

"I've got a guy you have to meet!" she said. "I heard him speak a while ago and he, he, he…"

Her expression changed, she paused, and then a humble look of gratitude spread across her face.

"He said some things I really needed to hear… right when I needed it most."

Carefully, I probed for more information. She revealed that she'd recently embarked on the long, treacherous journey of cancer treatment. It had been touch and go for a while. Her self-esteem and willingness to fight had been stretched to the breaking point. But now, she was in the clear, out of the darkness, and seeing life with a fresh set of eyes. She credited a guy named Robb with renewing her positive spirit, which made all the difference in her fight. Surely, I had to meet this guy.

Robb Holman and I both speak on business and leadership topics for a living. He's an extroverted extrovert who loves to extrovert, and I'm an introvert who likes to extrovert (I admit it).

Robb has a gift. You can feel it almost immediately. It's a rare trait that you encounter in only a few people in your lifetime. In simplistic terms, it's a positive force field. Once you get sucked in, you don't want to escape. Robb brings out the best in me when I'm with him, and I've watch how his force field can draw an entire room of people. It's obvious that he thinks uniquely, from the perspective of a kid's innocent curiosity, wonderment, and joy. He notices things and finds positive, reflective lessons in every encounter. Is it intentional? I wasn't sure how he managed to be that way consistently. How do you always live life in the moment like that? Then, I read this book, and it became clear. It comes from the Inside Out.

Robb is a leader. Why? Because most people (like me) would follow him anywhere. Isn't that the working definition of a leader? The forcefield is *that* compelling. He's uniquely qualified to teach others about leadership, and uses words, even though they're not necessary. Simply *living* the message is his most powerful expression of leadership.

Lead The Way will take you on a journey through the uncharted areas of your heart. I found myself facing the bare naked truth thanks to the potent questions posed in this book - things that I hadn't thought about in a long time, things that I was too lazy or afraid to ask myself. These questions needed to be asked, reflected upon, and ultimately answered with action. Such questions are catalysts for transformation in our lives.

Robb drives home the point that positive change comes down to accountability. It's less about what others should do, and all about what *you* can do to lead a life of purpose. This is the Inside Out Leadership approach – and it's sustainable because it uncovers the true you at your authentic best.

I wish I had known and incorporated the insights from *Lead The Way* 25 years ago. If you're an entrepreneur or new to a leadership role at any level, take advantage of this. Get off to a great start and build the neurological pathways that lead to consistent results. If you've been stuck and want a fresh batch of encouragement along with the confidence to lead in a liberated way, this book will be your guide. Each chapter will challenge you to take practical steps to act upon your vision for success. Robb unpacks the most thought-provoking leadership concepts, providing a relevant guide to articulate and incorporate them into your personal repertoire. They include Purpose, Happiness, Joy, Gratitude, Motivation vs Inspiration, Vision, and Values. You'll come away with a full game plan for living intentionally, and a comprehensive communication plan for your business.

It's clear that Robb wrote *Lead the Way* from his heart. And like me, you will feel the positive forcefield in his wisdom and encouragement. This book is an expression of Robb living out his life purpose. He is here to help guide others and lead the way from the inside out. It will make all the difference in your purpose discovery journey.

So what are you waiting for? Dive in!

Steve Van Valin,
CEO Culturology
www.culturologyUSA.com

INTRODUCTION

IN A 2014 SURVEY by Deloitte University Press, nearly 90% of workers interviewed admitted that they were not excited about their careers. Business owners and leaders aren't too far behind at 80%. As a result of this lack of professional engagement, a Gallup poll estimated that the U.S. alone wastes $500 billion each year in lost productivity! With this undeniable truth hanging over our heads, work environments have become more like stagnant ponds than flowing rivers.

Do you know *why*?

The main reason is plain and simple: a lack of purpose and passion in the workplace. A rigid separation exists between one's personal and professional life.

What's even more alarming is that nearly 80% of organizations *know* they have an engagement problem. Concerned leaders have employed a variety of techniques in attempts to motivate their team members. Such strategies have given us decent results, but not nearly the transformational change needed to maximize workplace performance. These approaches almost always operate from the outside in.

Thankfully, there is a better way to transform workplace culture and conquer low engagement rates once and for all – a way that empowers leaders to inspire and invigorate their teams rather than trying to squeeze productivity out of them. That's where Inside Out Leadership comes in.

Inside Out Leadership doesn't start with those you lead; it starts with YOU as the leader. In doing so, it closes the engagement gap, creates focus in your organization, and maximizes your time and profits.

Over the last 20 years, I have successfully led countless business owners, executives, and leaders through my exclusive and proprietary method of Inside Out Leadership™ Coaching. Through this method, I help leaders learn how to connect with their unique life purpose and find success in a way they never expected - from the inside out!

I'm excited to present to you my results-driven and purposeful Inside Out Leadership™ principles as a practical guide to transform your leadership and help you *Lead the Way*!

Robb Holman
Holman International, Founder & CEO
<u>www.robbholman.com</u>

PART I

Foundations for Inside Out Leadership™

Chapter 1
It's All About Perspective!

"When you change the way you look at things, the things you look at change." - Wayne Dyer

At the ripe age of twenty-one, I launched my first business – a motivational basketball program for youth. Just two years later, I experienced one of the greatest joys in my twenty years as an entrepreneur, raising $45,000 in seed money through private investors to purchase a brand of performance basketball clothing. I was a twenty-three-year-old with two businesses under my belt, pursuing a lifelong dream. It was truly a time for celebration. I had a prized opportunity to take my love of basketball and make a wider impact than I ever imagined. This sense of purpose has fueled me ever since.

Each day of our lives is to be enjoyed, celebrated, and filled with a unique sense of purpose - even in the workplace. I can't help but notice how many professionals are more passionate about weekends and planned vacations than coming to work on a daily basis. Typically, their favorite day of the week is Friday and their least favorite is Monday. Built into this lifestyle is a separation of one's personal and professional lives.

But what would happen if business owners and leaders began to align their career with their life purpose? In other words, you'd have an experiential understanding of why you exist, and you'd connect it to your career. Is it possible to live this life of purpose and passion all the time, regardless of your circumstances? My answer is a resounding "YES!" Imagine if wherever you go, whatever you do, you are filled with a genuine sense of purpose every step of the way.

How do you live your life to the fullest and positively influence those you encounter every day? How do you maximize your effectiveness and leave a lasting imprint throughout your life and business?

The answer lies in PERSPECTIVE!

Cultivating and maintaining a healthy perspective is one of most liberating practices in the entire world. Think about it: Two people can get the same email from their boss, yet each individual will read that email differently. One may interpret it through the lens of constructive criticism. Thus, the learner in them now knows how to improve their performance for a future promotion. Meanwhile, the other person may take offense to the email and assume that their job is in jeopardy. How is it that two individuals look at the same exact content and paint two completely different pictures? This is the power of perspective.

Here is another example. What do you see when you look at the following image?

Do you see a woman's face or a man playing the saxophone? Which one did you see first?

Over the years, I have tried the latest and greatest techniques and strategies to improve myself and to help those in my sphere of influence. These efforts translated into some positive results, but fell short of the transformational change I knew was possible. This is the crux of the issue. **We fall into the trap of trying to "fix" the outside in order to "fix" the inside.** But there's a better way! Instead of working from the outside in, how about discovering or rediscovering what is already in you and letting it out?

Living and leading from the inside out begins by making subtle, yet life-changing internal perspective shifts that lead to long-term vibrancy and sustainability. Here are some additional "inside out" perspective shifts that can turn your world upside down - or should I say, inside out!

Why Self-Discovery Outperforms Self-Help

"Humpty Dumpty sat on a wall. Humpty Dumpty had a great fall. All the king's horses and all the king's men couldn't put Humpty Dumpty back together again."

Now doesn't that bring back childhood memories?

Aside from nostalgia, there's something else to be found in this classic nursery rhyme - a profound metaphor. Let's face it: We are not strangers to brokenness, living in a world that is rife with struggles, challenges, trials, and tribulations. Many of us are just going through the motions, suffering from depression, anxiety, and stress overload. The statistics are staggering. Approximately 1 in 5 adults in the U.S.—43.8 million or 18.5%—experience some form of mental illness in a given year. This includes anxiety disorders like post-traumatic stress disorder, obsessive-compulsive disorder, specific phobias, etc.

So what have we employed to address this epidemic?

Self-help!

Self-help is a $10 billion per year industry in the U.S. alone. Many people are repeat customers. This begs the question: How much good are these self-help materials actually doing?

Self-improvement books are chock full of detailed formulas and techniques that promise us happiness, weight loss, money, popularity, and more. Marketdata Enterprises projected a 6.1% average annual growth rate for the self-help industry beginning in 2012, suggesting this steady stream of content isn't going anywhere. But there are cracks forming in the success story of the self-help industry, with infomercial sales plummeting 40% from 2007-2011 and book sales dropping 20% since 2007. The U.S market for personal coaching, weight loss programs, and stress management programs also took a hit from 2009 to 2011. Are Americans waking up to the lack of results they're getting?

We are inundated with resources and advice promoting the latest surefire way to fix ourselves because, as they claim, we are broken. I am not against many of these resources, but I believe there is a better way than living out the Humpty-Dumpty nursery rhyme. It's called self-discovery.

From Self-Help to Self-Discovery!

Imagine a life in which you don't have to put yourself back together. Self-discovery is about embracing what feels right and acknowledging the seeds of greatness within you – even if that feeling of brokenness lingers.

When we rely on outside sources to put us back together like Humpty-Dumpty, the journey becomes more about striving, comparison, performance, and expectation. With self-discovery, it's all about rest, satisfaction, anticipation, and yes, even enjoyment. It's also about learning to appreciate who you are and celebrating the unique gift you are to the world.

Years ago, I tried to emulate another public speaker. I adopted some of his mannerisms, his preparation routine, and his style of communication. But instead of confidence, this led to major frustration and discouragement. I knew it wasn't quite right. *I* wasn't quite right.

That's when I embarked on the path of self-discovery. Learning more about my gifts allowed me to concentrate on my unique speaking and engagement qualities that make me who I am today. Why would I want to be anyone else in the world but me?

You can't leverage your unique qualities and capabilities if you don't know what they are. Furthermore, instead of trying to fix your weaknesses, you can tear down old ideologies and patterns of thinking. Dive deep inside yourself to identify the strengths that are there to make you exceptional and extraordinary. (We'll delve into this more later!)

Igniting your purpose is not about fixing problems. It's about building on your strengths - on what makes you unique. You're already great. In Chapter 6, you'll find out why.

The Important Distinction between Inspiration and Motivation and Why You Should Care

For many years, I believed that inspiration and motivation meant the same thing. But the more I thought about it, researched it, and truly became a student of people, the more I realized a critical distinction. It was this critical distinction that made a world of difference in how I came to understand leadership.

Merriam-Webster Dictionary defines the two words as follows:

- Inspiration - Something that makes someone want to do something, or that gives someone an idea about what to do or create.
- Motivation - The act or process of giving someone a reason for doing something.

Motivation is when people give us a reason to act, whereas inspiration is when a person reaches the point of *wanting* to act. So here's the question: As a leader, do you want to motivate or inspire? Or, to be blunt: Do you want to babysit people or empower people? Of course, there is a need for both motivation and inspiration in the world. But to lead effectively, knowing the difference is important, and acting on the difference is crucial.

Remember when we talked about self-help vs. self-discovery? Just as living from the inside out is more powerful than living from the outside in, inspiring is more powerful than motivating.

Best-selling author and motivational speaker, Simon Sinek frames it like this:

"When we communicate from the outside in, yes, people can understand vast amounts of complicated information - features and benefits and facts and figures. It just doesn't drive behavior. When we communicate from the inside out, we're talking directly to the part of the brain that controls behavior, and then we allow people to rationalize it with the tangible things we say and do. This is where gut decisions come from. It's why you can give someone all the facts and figures and they'll say that they know what the facts say, but it just doesn't 'feel' right."

When we try to motivate people with positive incentives, and perhaps even negative reinforcement, we are using outward tactics to try to pry into the heart (where real change takes place). This can work to some degree, but the effect is usually temporary.

When we inspire people, we're reaching their heart in a way that transforms them from the inside out. When people want to change because of a deep stirring in their heart, it's sustainable. With that shift comes long-term vibrancy.

There was a time in my life as a young business owner and leader when I consistently sought encouragement from others as my main source of motivation. As a founder and CEO of two businesses in my mid-twenties, I didn't have a ton of experience. This resulted in a deep desire to receive validation for my business decisions. Sometimes I'd get it; other times I wouldn't. So I became dependent on the encouragement of others to perform well. I was living from the outside in. Then, I had an epiphany.

I encountered a purpose-driven challenge that helped me understand that what I do does not define who I am. My basketball clothing business had reached an all-time low with social and financial difficulties. Up until this time, it was common for friends and colleagues to stop by my office to chat about personal challenges. But I began to tell our Executive Assistant that I was not available for drop-ins. This continued for a long time, and it was weird because I typically love people! Then one day when my Executive Assistant was out, I heard a friend's voice echo through the front door.

"Robb, are you here?"

As they shuffled around the main office looking for me, I sensed they were getting closer to my office. My door was malfunctioning and wouldn't shut all the way. As they approached, I knew they would notice that my door was cracked open and peak in, so I slipped behind it to hide. Standing on my tiptoes behind the door, I prayed they wouldn't find me and distract me from my important work. At that moment, I felt a nudge deep in my heart.

Look at yourself. Is this what it has come to?

In that moment, everything changed. Up until then, I was all about "getting things done" and seeking approval from others. But a deeper urge to start putting others before myself began to grow.

With motivation, I was looking for reasons to be a better me. I was dependent on others to improve my performance. Work came first and people came second. But becoming inspired helped me discover who I was from the inside out. As a natural byproduct, I was able to accomplish things that I never thought were possible. I spent more time with the people in my life who had personal and professional needs. This empowered all of us. In addition, our team became more focused and unified as work-life balance improved.

Are Joy and Happiness Really the Same?

Married by twenty-five, kids by thirty, single-family home with a white picket fence by thirty-five, and a secure job for one or both spouses by forty. Sound familiar? Oh, and don't forget the family Disney trip sometime before the oldest child turns 9.

In American culture, these are the traditional milestones we equate with happiness. Movies like *The Pursuit of Happiness* reinforce this notion, our own expectations support it, and other people's expectations ingrain it. People say, "That's just the way it's always been," with a shrug. But if we're not careful, we let this cultural momentum dictate what happiness is and what it means for us.

There are so many things in our society that we question: political issues, motives of people's hearts, etc. Yet we rarely question what truly satisfies the human spirit.

I recently heard a powerful metaphor to this very point:

A young man jumped in a river that flowed as far as the eye could see both ahead of him and behind him. The river flowed continuously and bustled with activity – people were making things, talking about things, helping one another, etc. No one seemed to care where the river was taking them. In fact, no one even questioned it. But one day, the young man found himself at a sandbar. He stepped outside of the river for the first time in twenty years. At that moment, he was astonished. The river was all he had known. Standing on the bank and watching the people busily float by, he realized that everyone - himself included - had a "river-only" perspective. Yet there was so much more. An entire world existed on the other side of the bank, but no one cared to explore it. It did not mean that the river was bad. It just meant that there were opportunities that now awaited him that he never would've imagined!

I believe that the river is happiness and the world beyond the bank is Joy. Although happiness is great, it is dependent upon our circumstances. In a sense, happiness is conditional.

"If this thing happens, then I will be happy."

"If I pursue this job, this relationship, this promotion, this goal, and it doesn't happen, then what? Will I still be happy?"

Here is another way to think about it. Suppose you had all the money in the world and could eat at the finest restaurants, but you didn't know about anything beyond a generic diner down the street from your house. Even if their food was good, you'd be missing out on a lifetime of variety.

Happiness feeds on expectation. Joy goes deeper. It is not dependent upon circumstances, goals, or aspirations. Joy is simply a gift with no strings attached. Not one. It's an unspeakable, unshakable, and enduring anchor, regardless of where we end up.

A happy person may see the glass half full, but a joyful person always sees it overflowing. In Part II, we'll look at how Inside Out Leadership directly facilitates the transition from happiness to Joy.

Practical Step: Things That Really Matter

Let's say it again: It's all about perspective! If we desire a powerful and positive outlook on life, it begins with awareness and an embracing of the things that really matter. We must remember that we are already valuable, not broken, and that Joy starts with one courageous step out of the river.

We live such fast-paced lives that reflection, focused presence, and silence are usually absent. So take a minute to contemplate and answer this question: If you only had six months to live, how would you spend it? Imagine that you have no limitations in those final months - no worries, no pain, no financial constraints, and your energy level is sufficient. Really consider it.

What would you do?

CHAPTER 2
Redefining Success

"Success comes from knowing that you did your best to become the best that you are capable of becoming." - John Wooden

SUCCESS IS ONE OF those words that we are so accustomed to hearing that we've become numb to what it really means - or what it could mean. When you hear the word "success," what immediately comes to mind? There are so many concepts that we automatically tack a definition onto, but does that make them true?

It's always useful to step back from a commonly-used word, phrase, or statement to see if it is correct, or at least to see if it resonates with you. In the Western world, we operate from a way of thinking that is categorical in nature. Everything has its place. Everything exists in nice and neat color-coded folders with labels that help us define things.

The Eastern world, however, is much more holistic. Researchers from opposite hemispheres came together for a research study that looked at how East Asians and European Americans processed sensory information. They expected that human processing wouldn't vary, despite the geographical differences. But instead, they found that Americans spent more time focusing on the featured object in a scene, while Asians took in the entire picture. Asian participants switched their focus from the background to the foreground repeatedly.

Rather than boxing things into categories, Easterners observe how everything works together. There is a flow, a rhythm, and a harmony in which life is to be lived. It is through this wider lens that words can be defined and understood. In order to gain true perspective on success, it is important to keep this in mind to *Lead the Way*!

You Are a Success without Doing Anything

I've had the opportunity to coach many sales professionals. The primary reason I get hired is that they take rejection too personally. They hear "no" so often that they adopt a belief that says it must be them and not the product or service they sell.

Consider inside sales, where people makes up to two hundred cold calls per day and only hear about five people say "yes." The other one hundred and ninety-five people hang up on them, spew a few choice words, or politely act interested only to decline after a lengthy conversation. It's no wonder sales professionals get worn out!

But what does this have to do with your success?

We can easily let job performance, circumstances, choices, roles, and responsibilities become our identity. The moment we allow that to happen, we enter into a vicious cycle of limitation. Maintaining a healthy mindset about who you are is vital when it comes to your overall vibrancy and long-term sustainability. If we do not know who we are, we go through life absorbing negativity and taking too many things personally. We will talk more about this in Chapter 4.

Do you believe that you are unique, significant, and have a voice that people need to hear? Is your love of life contagious?

Show me someone who believes they have value, and I'll show you someone who will achieve a lot in their lifetime.

This leads us to the next question: What does success really mean?

How You Define Success Will Define You

Everyone's opinion of success takes on different forms. Do you think success means making a certain amount of money, having a high level of prestige, gaining acceptance from your peers, or buying a new home?

There's nothing wrong with these things in and of themselves, but there can be more to the meaning of success. I have found that the way you define success will ultimately define you. If you focus your time and energy on fleeting things, your heart won't be satisfied for long. But if you center your attention and effort on things that last, your heart will stay filled.

As a young entrepreneur, I learned this the hard way. I bent my heart toward getting my name in the newspaper, making a lot of money, gaining the approval of others, buying a better car, and getting accolades.

Unknowingly, I had defined success in these ways, and it then defined who I was. I slowly began prioritizing things over people, and it wasn't working in my favor on the inside. Sure, there was financial growth... but at what personal expense? I was tired, I was straining, and I was in desperate need of a new perspective like we discussed in Chapter 1.

This inner struggle to define success led me to a deeper understanding of the concept. The purpose of my business was to help people, not to acquire popularity.

What kind of impact could I have by giving my heart to people and my mind to business?

Suddenly, it hit me. My business had never really been about me. It was about the profound impact I could make through my work. In that moment of truth I felt an immense sense of liberation. My life purpose to be of service to others became clearer.

As a result of this realization, I now define success as the number of lives I can positively impact - not the number of things I can buy. When you live to serve others, tremendous blessings come your way.

Now knowing that success can define you, it's time to get the upper hand and redefine your success.

My Success Journey Highlights

Basketball has always been a great love in my life. Some of my earliest childhood memories include playing in basketball games against players much older and better than me. Oddly, I enjoyed getting roughed up, having the ball thrown back in my face, and being out-muscled and challenged to the core. How exciting! It's not the kind of situation you would typically call "successful." But being the underdog altered my perspective. It made me strong from within, which greatly shaped the way I approach basketball. The game came easily to me - much more easily than other hobbies, sports, and extracurricular activities. I experienced Joy as I played the game. As a result, it didn't feel like work to practice hard and see the fruits of my labor. But where did my love of basketball fit into my life's purpose?

I still remember sitting on my mom's porch shortly after graduating from college.

What am I going to do with my life?

Does my predicament sound familiar? I was reading the book, *What Color Is Your Parachute?* - a great resource that helps people figure out which career path is most suitable for them. Soon after this, I began my corporate job search. For me, as for many, it seemed like the next logical step after graduating from college with a business degree.

After trudging through various sales and marketing interviews, the notion that I was born to start something was affirmed. As far back as I could remember, I was always initiating projects, influencing people, and taking others with me on my journey!

Why should now be any different?

As I prayed and thought about what I wanted to do with my life, I was challenged to consider that which brings me great joy. At age 21, the three major areas of my life were basketball, inspiring people, and empowering the next generation of kids to move toward their ultimate goals. I saw no reason to wait five, let alone thirty years to do what I loved. So I decided to combine all three of these things and start a business! Sounds reasonable, right? Although I had a business education, I had no idea how to begin besides going after the things that made me passionate.

The more I pondered the possibilities, the more passionate I became. I quickly devised a business plan, recruited my older brother, rallied startup money, and hit the ground running. The plan was to use basketball as a vehicle to instill or reinforce life-changing values into children aged 5-14 through motivational basketball camps, clinics, leagues, instructional coaching, and speaking. Our business grew quickly, and within a few years, we were working with more than 500 kids through our programs each year. We also created a mentoring system with our junior and senior counselors and coaches.

I am so grateful that this initial experience catapulted me into a life of serial entrepreneurship, founding or co-founding 9 different businesses over the past 20 years. My personal experience of stepping up and doing what I loved truly ignited my entrepreneurial journey.

Practical Step: Your Success Journey

Answer the following 3 questions to activate your success journey:

1. How would you currently define success?
2. What are some of your success journey highlights thus far?
3. Are there any passion areas from your past that serve as a sign post pointing "This Way"?

It's important to remember that you are on a path that will change your life. Get excited about the opportunity to redefine what success looks like based on what really matters to you.

CHAPTER 3

The Authentic You

"Authenticity is a collection of choices that we have to make every day. It's about the choice to show up and be real. The choice to be honest. The choice to let our true selves be seen." - Brené Brown

"BE REAL."

"Stay true to yourself."

"Don't forget where you came from."

These are all familiar sayings, particularly in American culture. But do we practice what we preach? If we believe so strongly in authenticity, why do we see so little of it? It is one thing to put on a facade and another to let people know who you truly are. In a world that seems to become shallower under the influence of technology, I feel that we as people are losing our depth too. Our opinions of ourselves are shrinking, along with our opinions of what others think of us. As a result, there are shallower, **less authentic** relationships than ever before. Pastor Dr. Bob Moorehead masterfully explains this phenomenon:

"The paradox of our time in history is that we have taller buildings but

shorter tempers, wider freeways, but narrower viewpoints. We spend more but have less, and we buy more, but enjoy less. We have bigger houses and smaller families, more conveniences, but less time. We have more degrees but less sense, more knowledge, but less judgment, more experts, yet more problems, more medicine, but less wellness.

We drink too much, smoke too much, spend too recklessly, laugh too little, drive too fast, get too angry, stay up too late, get up too tired, read too little, watch TV too much, and pray too seldom.

We have multiplied our possessions but reduced our values. We talk too much, love too seldom, and hate too often. We've learned how to make a living, but not a life. We've added years to life but not life to years. We've been all the way to the moon and back, but have trouble crossing the street to meet a new neighbor. We conquered outer space but not inner space. We've done larger things, but not better things.

We've cleaned up the air, but polluted the soul. We've conquered the atom, but not our prejudice. We write more but learn less. We plan more but accomplish less. We've learned to rush, but not to wait. We build more computers to hold more information, to produce more copies than ever, but we communicate less and less.

These are the times of fast foods and slow digestion, big men and small character, steep profits and shallow relationships. These are the days of two incomes but more divorce, fancier houses, but broken homes. These are the days of quick trips, disposable diapers, throwaway morality, one night stands, overweight bodies, and pills that do everything from cheer, to quiet, to kill. It is a time when there is much in the showroom window and nothing in the stockroom. A time when technology can bring this letter to you, and a time when you can choose either to share this insight or to just hit delete."

Do you want to be rich? Then find one person in your life with whom you can be authentic with no fear of judgment - one person who can be present for you and truly listen to what you have to say, one person with whom you can have a true bond and reciprocate. Rich indeed!

Now, I'm not saying that you have to spill the beans about everything with everyone. Just be liberated enough to be yourself. What would life be like if, regardless of the circumstances and the people, you were comfortable just being you? What would life be like if you led your business from this place?

We Are Born to Explore

We are natural explorers. We always have been, and we always will be. The YouTube video entitled, "We Are the Explorers" by NASA's Johnson Space Center sums it up nicely:

"We are the explorers. We have a need to find what is out there. It is a drive inside each and every one of us, the drive to wonder, to push the boundaries, and to explore. We expanded across our lands, settling new frontiers. We took to the oceans and learned that we could cross treacherous expanses in the pursuit of discovery, and then we took to the skies and flew. But that wasn't enough. We left the planet and redefined what was possible. We flew in space; we walked in space. What once was a melodramatic flight of fantasy became reality.

Then, a new generation of spaceships captured hearts and minds for three decades and helped build a castle in the sky that is our lasting home in space. We have always looked up. For centuries, we wondered what was on the other side of the sky, and we have begun to answer that question. We have learned that all the exploration humankind has achieved is only a beginning. Right now, men and women are working on the next steps to go farther than we have ever gone before. New vessels will carry us, and new destinations await us. We don't know what new discoveries lie ahead, but this is the very reason we must go."

There is one very short question that children ask far more than any other. Do you know what it is?

"Why? Mommy, why is the sky blue? Daddy, why don't things fall up?" Sometimes the question comes with tears, sometimes with a straight face, sometimes with a whiny voice, and sometimes with a heart eager to learn.

As a parent of three young children, I'm often tempted to respond to my children's "whys" with, "Because I said so!" My response usually comes from a place of annoyance or frustration. Such responses, when repeated, can crush a child's spirit of exploration and curiosity. For this reason, my wife and I have made a commitment that no matter how tired and frustrated we might feel, we provide explanations to our children.

When we revive our spirit of exploration, we find a place where self-discovery is at its greatest and authenticity comes alive! There's something simple, beautiful, creative, powerful, and significant about letting the kid inside of us out.

I realized how strongly exploration guides us when I attended a leadership conference in Orlando, Florida with a few close friends. Not long into the four-day conference, we saw on the news that a brush fire was burning close to where we were staying. Sure enough, our sense of exploration kicked in.

"I wonder how far away it is. Let's go and see how close we can get without catching on fire!" (Great idea, right?)

I remember calling my wife and saying, "Karen, guess what we're planning on doing today?"

After I told her, Karen replied, "I don't think that's such a great idea, Robb."

"Alright, I'll talk to the guys and see if they'll reconsider..." I responded.

With my wife's help, I became the voice of reason, but my friends were still bent on going. To be honest, so was I!

And so we were off, driving toward the raging fire. Policeman, fireman, and other officials were teaming up to make sure maniacs like us would not be able to get anywhere close to the flames. We drove past closed roads and barricades that blocked our goal.

My adrenaline was pumping, and the spirit of discovery was alive and well in me. We drove as far as we could and then started off on foot. Though grown men, we were like ten-year olds on a slapdash adventure. When we reached as far as we could on foot, we saw the flames licking up a couple hundred yards away. I don't know if you've ever been close to a brush fire, but it consumes everything in its path. From the woods, we heard the roar of the blaze and saw its engulfing power firsthand. We found an embankment from which to watch the fire as it quickly spread toward us. The sound was getting louder, the heat was getting hotter, and it finally registered that things could get serious.

With a firm tone I said, "Guys, it's time. We need to move now!"

I couldn't believe what I heard next.

"No man, we're going to stay a little bit longer." Shocked at their willingness to take that risk, I started heading back on my own. Just minutes later, I realized that the other four guys were following my lead. Coming out of this eye-opening experience safely taught me three things:

1.) We are born explorers.
2.) Listen to the wife more often!
3.) We all need to continue exploring and discovering to find the hidden joy and sense of adventure our hearts long for.

T.S. Eliot expresses it like this: "We must not cease from exploration. And the end of all our exploring will be to arrive where we began and to know that place for the first time."

Now that I've shared my crazy brush fire experience, reflect on some adventures you've had. It doesn't have to be a situation as extreme as mine. Simply think of something that really stretched you. Maybe you had an adventure as a child, or maybe it was very recent. Can you recall how it made you feel? Did you feel alive, reinvigorated, courageous, or scared? We all explore in hopes of harnessing these raw emotions.

It's one thing to explore the natural world, but it's another thing entirely to explore our hearts. Similarly, many small business owners give their time, resources, and energy to the outside world while paying little attention to their inner world. We are often expert givers, but when it comes to receiving, we don't do so well.

Part of the reason for this imbalance is that when we intentionally look deep within, we find ourselves in a vulnerable and transparent place - a place that is often very uncomfortable. Many people don't like to explore there because they are afraid of what they might find. Many leaders are fearful of self-discovery.

There is a similar phenomenon that occurs in many people (mostly men). They avoid their primary physician for years because they are afraid of what problems might be revealed. But wouldn't you want to know what's going on so you could do something about it? Now, this chapter is about authenticity, so I'll share something that may surprise you... I was one of those guys! I had not been to my doctor for about 7 years. To my credit, I had some blood tests during that time, but never an annual physical. Eventually, after some encouragement from my wife and others, I went to the doctor. After that appointment, I knew my physical body far better than I had in a long time! I was referred to a couple of specialists and followed up with them too. Since then, I feel like I know myself again. I gained confidence in my body and learned practical takeaways to remain healthy. Another powerful thing I learned was that the choice to see or not see a doctor not only impacts me, but my family, friends, business partners, and others in my sphere of influence. The self-discovery process works just the same.

Going From Outside to Inside Exploration

Self-discovery is where the Inside Out Leadership™ Check-Up really comes in handy. Consider it like a thorough doctor's appointment – for the heart and mind. (At the end of this book, you'll be given a special code to take the test and see how you're doing as an Inside Out leader.)

We have to see the value within to truly understand our own personal significance. Each of us is distinct from every other human being on planet Earth. Much of the world is telling you who you should be, what you should look like, how you should act, etc. But rather than following external rules, you can lead yourself down a road of excitement, anticipation, and expectancy. Good things await you on this journey, and they do not just exist for the sake of an aha moment. They exist to transform you for life. These discoveries will have you exclaiming, "*This is who I was designed to be!*"

Wow, talk about authenticity! When you understand who you are and who you're not, you'll find purity, joy, and humility because you did nothing at all to earn the gift that you are.

Self-Discovery Helps You Operate in Rest

If self-help easily sweeps us off our feet with an unhealthy striving to fix ourselves, then self-discovery gives us a much-needed rest. Think about it: Out of the billions of people that have ever lived, there is no other you.

Look at your strengths, passions, life milestones, and distinct qualities – including the heartaches, hurts, and pains that have actually made you who you are today. Just like me, you sit here with a story to tell.

Years ago, I had a vivid dream that radically changed my life. No, I didn't eat too much before bed and have one of those goofy and nonsensical dreams as a result. Rather, it was more real than me sitting here writing this book. I suddenly found myself climbing a flagpole thousands of feet in the air. As I exerted every ounce of strength trying to get to the top, the pole was rapidly falling toward the ground. It reminded me of the striving and exhaustion I felt back in elementary school trying to climb a rope from one knot to the next. I was all arms and legs with minimal upper body strength! It was torturous, just like the sensation in the dream.

All of a sudden, I heard a voice say to me, "You can expend all your energy trying to reach the top, or you can completely let go. Either way, you're going to die." When I heard this, I immediately stopped climbing. That voice was my turning point. I could keep struggling in vain or just let go. What do you think I did?

I let go! And it was the most liberating feeling of peace and rest I've ever felt in my life.

An instant later, I blacked out and awoke on the ground, alive, with that same feeling of rest and peace flooding through me. I said no to striving and chose rest. I've got to tell you, my life has never been the same since that vivid dream... It's all about perspective, right?

If you were wondering throughout this Chapter, "Well what's the alternative to self-discovery, Robb?" The alternative is what I was doing at the start of my dream: struggling to reach the top of something that would soon smash to the ground. The flag pole represented a routine and mundane life, not to mention, a futile and painful existence. To be completely honest with you, life is too short and too important to go through the motions. Rather than blindingly charging toward the "top," why not indulge in some personal exploration? Are you with me?

Don't Just Give the Message, Be the Message!

Have you ever listened to a speaker who nailed every speaking point in their presentation? Their PowerPoint was near perfect, and their closing statement was the pinnacle of the presentation. However, they didn't inspire you or lead you to real action.

On the flip side, have you ever listened to a speaker who presentation wasn't as polished, but they spoke from a very deep place in their heart? In other words, they spoke with firm conviction, passion, and life experience, luring you to the edge of your seat.

A message is more caught than taught. If you speak from the mind, you will receive mindful responses, but if you speak from the heart you will get hearts on fire! Methodist Church Founder, John Wesley was known for saying, "Light yourself on fire with passion, and people will come for miles to watch you burn." As people watch you burn, they will naturally catch on fire. This is the essence of authenticity.

Do you remember the 2010 movie, *The Book of Eli*, starring Denzel Washington? Eli possessed a book that contained ancient wisdom believed to have the intrinsic power to control people. Not surprisingly, everyone wanted to get their hands on the book, and eventually it was stolen. However, while the book was in his possession, Eli meditated on the book, lived with the book, slept with the book, talked about the book, and fully experienced the book. Over time, he no longer needed the book in his possession.

Eli *became* the message and no longer needed anything outside of himself. Now, it's your turn to become your message.

Practical Step: Creating Your Brand

Uncovering the authentic you is all about being comfortable and confident in your skin. A fun way to exercise getting comfortable and confident is to create your brand. There are many celebrities, entertainers, professional athletes, and big-time business executives who have personal brands. Names such as Oprah Winfrey, Ryan Seacrest, Lebron James, Serena Williams, and Tony Robins come to mind. Just by answering the following questions, you'll take a step closer to the authentic you.

1. What is your personal tagline? Come up with a word, a phrase, or a statement that best describes the message deep within that you want to get across.
2. Who is your target audience? These people are your ultimate bulls-eye - the ones you have a primary interest in reaching. Remember that you will always reach people outside of your target audience, but you still want to be intentional about who you aim to reach.
3. What guest(s) would you have on your first public TV show and why? These people best exemplify and reflect your message and would help you reach your target audience.

CHAPTER 4

Overcoming the Obstacle

"Get unstuck quickly. Do something that will get you a small win. That builds momentum and gives you the confidence to make bigger and wiser decisions." - Hani Mourra

ONE QUESTION THAT I am frequently asked is, "Do you ever have a bad day?" It's fascinating to watch people's expressions as they eagerly await my response!

I always try to respond with another question: "How would you define a bad day?" Usually people describe a day that started off on the wrong foot and kept snowballing out of control. Nothing seems to go right all day long. Frustration leads to more frustration and discouragement leads to more discouragement, resulting in a slippery slope of emotions that yields a bad day. I'm sure you've heard the saying, "When it rains, it pours!"

Please know this: It doesn't have to be that way.

Case in point, my son and I recently went to get haircuts together. It was pouring rain. Torrential downpour might be a better way to describe that Saturday afternoon. But despite the heavy rain, we ventured out to make the most of a father-son bonding opportunity. We parked and made a b-line for the barbershop. As we abruptly left the car, I noticed the automatic lock wasn't working, but I didn't have time to go back. In the back of my mind I thought that it was unusual, but I still took the chance.

After 30 minutes, our haircuts were finished and the storm had subsided. As we approached the car, I noticed that one of the doors was left open the entire time. Everything was soaking wet. In that moment, I almost slipped into an automatic negative reaction. But in the midst of the craziness, I chose not to go down the path of "how could I let this happen?"

Rather than beating myself up, I searched for the positives amid the whirlwind of potential problems: My son stepped up and helped like I've never seen before. We had a wet vacuum at home that aided tremendously in the cleanup. My wife and kids were so understanding. There were so many positive elements to a situation that easily could have ruined my day. If I allow for that downward thought spiral, a bad day can lead into a bad week, month, year, and even lifetime!

Personally, I've learned the secret of not letting a bad moment turn into other bad moments that become a bad day. This method involves mastering your thoughts and emotions.

The Power Between Our Ears

I love what James Clear says in his Huffington Post article, "The Science of Positive Thinking: How Positive Thoughts Build Your Skills, Boost Your Health, and Improve Your Work."

"Play along with me for a moment. Let's say that you're walking through the forest and suddenly a tiger steps onto the path ahead of you. When this happens, your brain registers a negative emotion — in this case, fear.

Researchers have long known that negative emotions program your brain to do a specific action. When that tiger crosses your path, for example, you run. *The rest of the world doesn't matter. You are focused entirely on the tiger, the fear it creates, and how you can get away from it. In other words, negative emotions narrow your mind and focus your thoughts. At that same moment, you might have the option to climb a tree, pick up a leaf, or grab a stick — but your brain ignores all of those options because they seem irrelevant when a tiger is standing in front of you. This is a useful instinct if you're trying to save life and limb, but in our modern society we don't have to worry about stumbling across tigers in the wilderness. The problem is that your brain is still programmed to respond to negative emotions in the same way — by shutting off the outside world and limiting the options you see around you.*

For example, when you're in a fight with someone, your anger and emotion might consume you to the point where you can't think about anything else. Or, when you are stressed out about everything you have to get done today, you may find it hard to actually start anything because you're paralyzed by how long your to-do list has become. Or, if you feel bad about not exercising or not eating healthy, all you think about is how little willpower you have, how you're lazy, and how you don't have any motivation. In each case, your brain closes off from the outside world and focuses on the negative emotions of fear, anger, and stress — just like it did with the tiger. Negative emotions prevent your brain from seeing the other options and choices that surround you. It's your survival instinct."

As with any challenge in life, progress begins with awareness! The mind is a powerful tool that can serve as your best friend or your worst enemy. The major battles in life emerge not from the people who have wronged you or the consequences that have seemingly come against you. The big showdown occurs between your ears.

Think of it like this: Your brain has downloaded a song and that song automatically plays on repeat 24/7. The question is, what song is it? What are the lyrics? What does the song say about you? Is the song true?

Through learning to bridge the gap between the rational and emotional parts of the brain, we can coax the mind into serving rather than tyrannizing us.

Travis Bradberry and Jean Greaves, authors of *Emotional Intelligence 2.0*, explain it like this: *"The physical pathway for emotional intelligence starts in the brain, at the spinal cord. Your primary senses enter here and must travel to the front of your brain before you can think rationally about your experience. But first they travel through the limbic system, the place where emotions are experienced. Emotional Intelligence requires effective communication between the rational and emotional centers of the brain."*

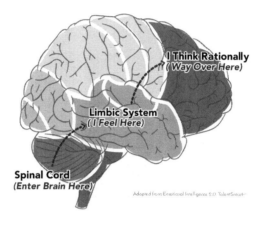

So, how do we learn to bridge the gap between the rational and emotional centers of our brain?

It Starts With a Thought

Recall the last time a negative thought popped into your mind. Was it during the course of your day, week, or during a certain period of your life? Sometimes they just seem to appear out of nowhere. They typically sound something like, "You're not good enough!" or "You don't have the confidence to handle that!"

The question isn't whether we get them, or how frequently we get them; it's what we do with them. If we give our power to that one negative thought, it becomes two. Two turns into three, and the next thing you know, we're bombarded with awful thoughts. That's how the downward spiral begins.

Because of life's complexities and the brain's vast capabilities, many of the thoughts that arise are not even true. Everything we consciously or subconsciously take in - like a hurtful thing a parent or sibling once said, or negative treatment from an authority figure - all of these experiences contribute to the negative perceptions that creep in and surprise us. It's all the more reason to be aware of what we're up against. Let's develop our awareness so that we don't fall into that pit of stinkin' thinkin!

What are some negative thoughts that consistently come up in your life? What perceptions are holding you back or falsely defining who you are?

Once you become aware of a negative thought, capture it! Speak truth to it. This process will need to be done several times until the new belief replaces the old one. We've got to replace that negative thought with at least three positive thoughts **that you believe**.

For instance, I'm engaged in a lot of different things in my life, which I love! I co-founded Agents of Efficiency, I'm the founder of Meeting House Ministries, and I get amazing opportunities to speak on my Inside Out Leadership philosophy around the world. Throughout my life, I've pursued unique opportunities and seen them bear fruit.

But to be completely honest, I still sometimes hear a tiny voice say, "You're not smart enough. You don't have the level of education to hang with these leaders! What could you possibly teach them that they don't already know?"

Over the years, this negative voice has reared its head. But the more I discover who I am and embrace my unique message, the better I get at overcoming it and moving forward. I am now aware of this negative voice and know how to appropriately deal with it so I can give more attention to the truth in my heart.

My response to the negative voice is, "I need to remember that I have a unique purpose. I'm thankful for my 20 years of personal and professional experience that has enabled me to share my ideas with confidence. I have an inspirational and proven message that burns so deep, leaders desperately need to hear it!"

These are three positive thoughts that I believe and repeat to myself to counteract the negative voice.

Not only is it critical to have awareness and replace the negative thoughts, but to also engage with trusted people in the process. This is absolutely necessary when the mind's barrage of negativity grows louder and stronger. The more intense the battle, the more deliberately we need to bring in reinforcements. Reach out to those that know you best and can encourage you, pray for you, or simply remind you of who you are!

When I confide in my trusted confidants I'll say something like, "Hey, what do you see in me? Do you think I have what it takes to bring my message to this particular group of leaders? Would you mind praying for me? Pray that I walk in courage, boldness, and freedom with my message?" Trust me, if I can be vulnerable and reach out for encouragement, you can too!

The Trap of Comparison Can Mess With Our Mind

If I only had more money like Bob, if I just had more opportunities like Sue, if I was more attractive like Christy, if I was cut like Ron, if I had a family like the Brown's, if I was taller like Dave, if I had more influence like Karen, if I was smarter like Megan, if I, if I, if I...

This is what I call "If I" syndrome. Unfortunately, it's easy to get sucked into this mentality without even realizing it. **Comparison thinking is a victim mindset rather than a victor mindset.**

When we are striving to be someone else, we stop embracing who we are. When we compare, we exhaust so much time and energy, subconsciously or consciously meditating on what someone else has. What if you channeled that time and energy into your very own self-discovery process and focused on maximizing your gifts and strengths?

You Are More Courageous Than You Think

Throughout my life I've seen people do some pretty outrageous things that left me thinking, "How in the world did they do that?" Have you ever come across someone that just seemed to be fearless in accomplishing things beyond human comprehension? If you are like me, you may have always put them in a special "superhuman" category.

Recently, a friend showed me a video of a guy named Danny MacAskill, a legend in trials cycling. This style of biking requires precision and control in extreme landscapes. In this particular clip, Danny rode his bike up the steep terrain of a mountain called The Ridge, calmly traversing the crags and massive rocks in his path. And of course, what goes up must come down - He then maneuvers himself back down the mountain without a single slip-up.

As I watched, I couldn't help but think that he was crazy. What would drive him to do such a perilous thing? However, the more I watched, the more inspired I became. It got me thinking about how my thoughts could have stopped me from doing the very things I was called to do. I remembered situations that were not quite as extreme as Danny's, but times when I clearly stepped outside of my comfort zone and displayed courage. In those moments, I captured the negative thought, replaced it with my trusted ones, and stepped outside of my comfort zone.

I was reminded of the first time I went to the Middle East to take a vision trip, the time I went up in a hot air balloon, had the guts to forgive a family member, or stepped back onto the basketball court after being out of the game for more than 6 years.

What is the most adventurous thing you've ever done? How were you stretched? Was it physical? Maybe you were pushed beyond your limits relationally, emotionally, spiritually, or even financially!

We are all braver than we know. We all possess a courageous spirit to do things that we never thought we could. Every time we step up and do something that stretches us, it's an invitation to begin living a courageous life - **get comfortable with the uncomfortable**.

We are capable of so much more than routine and ordinary tasks. We are made for the extraordinary... but it requires our participation.

Practical Step: What Are You Telling Yourself?

The primary obstacle is negative self-talk that creeps into our minds. We become what we believe.

Identify 2 recurring negative thoughts that are barriers keeping you from being all that you were created to be.

1.
2.

Identify 10 positive truths about you that will counteract these negative thoughts.

1.
2.
3.
4.
5.
6.
7.
8.
9.
10.

PART II

Core Convictions Of An Inside Out Leader

CHAPTER 5

Lead Yourself First

"Learning to lead yourself well is one of the most important things you'll ever do as a leader." - John C. Maxwell

WHILE OUT ON A walk, we've all noticed the two different types of dog owners. The first type has their dog well-trained. The dog exhibits perfect manners, following closely by the owner's side as they guide it where to go. Then there's the second type of dog owner, who often makes us snicker. Their dog takes *them* for a walk. Eagerly pulling far ahead, the dog darts in every direction while the owner simply tries to keep up. If not for the leash, the dog would be long gone! The second type of dog owner relinquishes their power, allowing the dog to be the leader in the relationship.

What decisions have you made, or relinquished, regarding leadership in your sphere of influence?

Leading yourself first means not allowing life to lead *you* - not allowing yourself to be dragged along by a tether. Instead, you can take the initiative and choose your own direction.

If you're more familiar with the second dog owner's leadership style, don't fret. The good news is, you can change.

Help Yourself Before You Help Others

There's an old saying that you may be familiar with: "Freely you have received, freely give." What in the world does that mean? You can only give to others what you have first received. For example, have you ever been around someone that's anxious all the time? When you spend time with them, you start to feel drained and anxious too. Nowadays, we even have a term for them: energy vampires. It's as if they can suck all the positive energy right out of you.

Thankfully, there's a flip side to this energy transfer. You've probably been around someone who is so full of joy that it naturally overflows onto others. It's not an act; it's simply who they are. You're always happy to spend time with them because they make you feel so great. You laugh more, smile more, and start walking with a bounce in your step. They are a breath of fresh air. Quite the opposite of an energy vampire, these people are energy *givers*!

We can only give to others what we have received. The big question is: What are you consistently receiving in your life? Whatever it is, that is also what you will give!

A lot of business owners and leaders are exceptional givers. You give your time, resources, energy, and service to people that trust and depend on you. **But from what place are you giving?**

Truthfully, it doesn't take long for givers to reach the point of burnout. Oftentimes, they are already burnt out and don't even realize it. If you are sidelined by exhaustion, unable to function in a healthy and productive way, how can you possibly assist others in a meaningful way?

It is extremely noble to give all you can. However, we must keep our future in mind. If you want to be vibrant and serving for years to come, it starts with honoring and serving yourself!

Think of the last time you boarded an airplane. Your flight attendant probably demonstrated how to use an oxygen mask and instructed you to secure your mask first before helping those around you. This surprises many people, and some are even resistant to it because it seems selfish. However, if you don't follow this rule, you won't be able to assist anyone anyway. If you don't attach your mask properly, you may quickly pass out, especially if the inside of the plane depressurizes rapidly. How much help can you provide when you are unconscious? You guessed it...zilch!

In order to be the kind of leader that models courage and helps others discover and live out their potential with joy, you'll need to receive that same thing *first*!

Let's look at the practical steps to get you there and help you *Lead the Way*.

Balance is Key

Many scholars and theologians would say that human beings are made up of 3 parts: spirit, soul, and body. Each component is unique, yet works in harmony to make up the wholeness of you. Leading yourself first is about getting back to the basics of self-care in all 3 areas.

First, let's briefly talk about the spiritual aspect of who we are. I like to define the spiritual as the deepest place in you that words can't even describe. Its runs deeper than your emotions and taps into the very essence of your existence - a place where purpose is ignited, vision is birthed, and experiential understanding that your life matters is gained.

What are you doing to nurture that spiritual dynamic in your own life?

For me, I have a personal relationship with God that I am committed to nurturing every day. I talk to Him, listen to Him, thank Him, worship, and learn new things about Him every day. My ongoing relationship with God creates a life of vibrancy, refreshment, and renewal. How about you? Do you have consistent time to reflect, meditate, or pray?

Next is our soul, which can be defined as our mind, will, emotions, and imagination. Our mind needs to be sharpened, our will needs to be tested, our emotions need to be balanced, and our imagination needs to be stretched. Think of the things you already engage in (or would like to engage in) that feed your soul. What is fun for you? What stirs you up, expands, or refreshes you? Maybe it's deep conversations with friends, doing something artistic, or reading a really thought-provoking book. When we engage in these kinds of healthy activities, they "feed the soul."

One of the many things I consistently engage in that feeds my soul is deep conversations with friends on topics that interest us. These talks challenge me and help me gain a better understanding of the people and the world around me.

The third and final aspect is the body, our "earth suit." Now, we all know that anything with moving parts needs regular maintenance to minimize wear and tear and ensure smooth operation and longevity. Our bodies are no less important. If we take our cars in for regular oil changes and inspections, shouldn't we pay the same, if not more respect to our bodies? So many leaders are running on fumes because they neglect their bodies.

Do you maintain a healthy diet? What about a proactive plan for incorporating the basic food groups? Drinking half your body weight of water (in ounces) per day is key!

How about exercise? I know this can look different for each person, but staying committed is what matters. You may enjoy walking, running, lifting weights, yoga, spin class, basketball, etc. I would not be able to do what I do if I didn't consistently exercise. Playing basketball for a number of years ingrained in me the desire to move – so much so that I've worked out for last twenty years without missing more than two weeks in a row. Selecting activities you enjoy is the best way to sustain your exercise habit.

Most physiologists agree that doing the following on a weekly basis is the minimum our bodies require for health and longevity:

- At least five days aerobic exercise for a duration of at least 30-minutes - Power walking is one of the best ways to satisfy this requirement.
- Two days of some form of weight training - The burpee with integrated push-ups is the best single load-bearing exercise you can do.
- One day of rest

You'll notice that the types of exercise I suggest require no equipment and no gym. So get moving!

Lastly, what about a good night's sleep? We know we should get a minimum of 7 hours per night for the sake of sanity. Beyond that, there are so many reasons to prioritize sleep it's astonishing. Sleep has been shown to reduce your risk of obesity, diabetes, and stroke, increase your capacity to learn, help you control emotions, and so much more.

As you can see, we are an integrated whole! The neglect of the spirit, soul, or body will negatively impact the other 2 areas. I'll give you a glimpse into my life with a funny story about how my spirit, soul, and body work together. Please laugh with me and not at me!

When I eat a snack after the kids go to bed, I tend to go for the salty treats instead of the sweet ones. (Isn't this the million-dollar question? Are you a sweet or salty snacker? Ha!) Anyways, when I reach for the bag of chips and start munching away, I always know when to stop to avoid overindulging. The majority of the time I steer clear of the dark side. My reasoning? If I cross the line and overindulge, it won't only affect my body, but my soul and spirit too. In other words, if I eat too much it is a discipline problem, not just a physical problem. I will not be as disciplined in my exercise, prayer life, or even receptivity to learning new things. When you pluck one string on a guitar, it causes the other strings to subtly vibrate too... Are you with me?

So when we find balance in one area of life, other areas naturally fall into balance. **Learning what we need, when we need it, and how often we need it helps us become good stewards of what we have.** When we learn to effectively lead ourselves first, we can give from that place of fullness. Remember, "Freely you have received, freely give." In essence, we become like a fire hydrant of vibrancy, passion, and life! As a result, you are a strong leader who positively influences the lives of those around you.

Maintain Your Balance by Guarding Your Boundaries

Leaders are an interesting breed. The more we mature in our leadership abilities, the more people want our time. However, you don't have to be ruled by the demands of others. In order to maintain balance, you must get used to saying NO! Trust me, it's a liberating lesson to learn.

Back in the day, I was the biggest people pleaser ever. I wanted to help people, so I guess my heart was in the right place. Still, I was very misguided. In many personal and professional conversations, I would find myself saying YES to almost everything that sounded good on the spot - whether it was being on this board or that board, mentoring people, helping a friend move... the list went on and on. A lack of intentionality and purpose made me unable to discern which things I should and shouldn't do. Thus, I wasn't able to fulfill all the commitments I made. As a person whose top core value is commitment, this ate me alive. I wasn't truly valuing other people, and more importantly, I wasn't valuing myself. It had everything to do with boundaries and balance.

Slowly but surely, I learned the importance of saying no. No doesn't mean I don't care. It just means that I care more about keeping my commitments and prioritizing what matters most. Every time you say no, you say yes to your priorities. When we let our yes be yes and our no be no, we value others and ourselves. So ask yourself: What are my genuine priorities in this season of my life? Once you determine your priorities you have a much better handle on your life.

Now remember, you will still have people and situations tugging at you and vying for that top position. But now, you'll have a filter to sift through opportunities and sort the yesses from the nos.

Rest Time

Every day in kindergarten, my classmates and I had rest time. We would take our little floor mats and space them apart in the classroom for about 20 minutes each day. Being the sensitive and happy-go-lucky five-year-old that I was, I would gravitate toward one of my closest classmates and start talking to them. I thought life was way too short to rest and that it was far more important to get to know people… but try telling that to a seasoned kindergarten teacher.

I've come a long way since then. Not only do I believe in the importance of rest, but I fully embrace it as a way to maintain balance and stay functional, clear, and focused.

The Sabbath principle is based on the notion of rest. The bible says that on 7th day, God rested. The prior 6 days were spent creating, and on the 7th day He enjoyed all that He had made. Now listen: If God had to rest, you better believe we do too! What would our lives look like if we were committed to taking one solid day off and not working at all? I can already hear some of you saying, "Well, I take off Saturdays and Sundays so I already live this principle!" But do you *really* rest and enjoy what you've created on those days? We can "take off" but still be consumed by thoughts, e-mails, phone calls, and messages pertaining to work.

There's a sales tactic that I find to be highly applicable here. It's called a pattern interrupt. Oftentimes in sales, you try to get through to the decision maker only to find out you must first pass the infamous "gatekeepers." These are the people that screen the calls, only allowing the "important" ones to get passed on. Of course, the gatekeeper receives similar solicitations all day long. They get used to the spiel, that is, until a skilled salesperson calls and speaks in a refreshing manner. This throws the gatekeeper off track. They interrupt the pattern the gatekeeper is accustomed to hearing, resulting in an opportunity to speak to the decision maker.

In the same way, a rest day is a pattern interruption. We need to change up our routine so that we stay fresh and engaged rather than bored and exasperated. Here is an exercise that will help you take this principle and put it into practice.

Practical Step: Have a Day All to Yourself

In the age of apps, fast food, text messages, microwaves, internet, drive-throughs, and express lanes, we're only ever rushing faster and faster. Sometimes the things that are supposed to save time only make us busier.

While most of us are pressured by expectations, deadlines, and consumerism, much of this stress is self-induced. Our own performance-driven mentalities contribute to the problem. The go-go-go lifestyle is difficult to escape for families that have kids with activities all over town, gym memberships that haven't been used nearly enough, and jobs where weekly sales goals drive profits. Without full awareness, these external drivers drag us under, and we pay the price.

To escape this cycle, we have to simply accept that we will be moving against the current.

We must stop letting our lives lead us and instead lead our lives. It begins by slowing down and taking stock of how you spend your time. You can take your life back one decision at a time. Start to discern what is not life-giving or not aligned with your purpose and priorities. What can be cut out or reduced? Create margins in your life so you have room to take advantage of new opportunities.

Then, consider this question: Imagine you had a day all to yourself, from the time you woke up to the time you went to sleep. What would you do?

You are free from roles, responsibilities, and everyone's expectations all day. Money is plentiful. (Yes, this might seem unrealistic, but let yourself dream.) What are the things that bring you the greatest delight?

Think of activities that are not work. Think of things that are totally play. How about reading, hanging out with friends, playing tennis, taking a long nap, going out to a favorite restaurant, catching a movie, finishing a personal project, or sitting on the beach?

Got it? **Now whatever it is, plan that day. Put it on the calendar at least once per quarter of the year.** On that day, turn your phone off and avoid emails! Doing these things is a tiny but groundbreaking step toward slowing down and taking back your life.

Chapter 6

Live a Life of Purpose

"Knowing your purpose gives meaning to your life." - Rick Warren

Isn't it amazing how much time we spend on activities that don't bring us any closer to our life's purpose? We have an innate sense that we were made for more, but we rarely think about it, only occasionally talk about it, and almost NEVER do anything about it! We all want to know why we are here and what we are here to do. And there's a reason for this: Research strongly indicates that living a life of purpose has physical, emotional, and relational benefits. It's as though our survival instinct drives us to find purpose.

A 2009 Japanese study showed that those who perceived themselves as having a purpose lived longer. Another study that year revealed that those who could name their purpose spent more time with their families, coworkers, and communities. In the book, *Resilience,* by Andrew Zolli, he even suggests that people living intentionally with purpose can "cognitively reappraise situations and regulate emotions, turning life's proverbial lemons into lemonade."

As we discussed in the introduction, disengagement is an epidemic in modern workplaces. The majority of workers are feeling bored and uninspired at work, and it is costing companies big money (lack of passion = a lack of innovation and thus lower revenue). What's worse, many leaders are feeling the same way, leading their teams from a place of malaise.

This is where Inside Out Leadership really comes in. When you lead from the inside out, you draw from your personal purpose and inject that enthusiasm into your work. Once your purpose is clarified, it begins to seep over into your professional life, no longer boxed into a tiny corner of your life.

So if you think discovering your life purpose is just some pie-in-the-sky idea to motivate you to act, I have a story that might change your perspective.

In the 2005 Super Bowl, my beloved Philadelphia Eagles experienced a devastating lost to the New England Patriots. It's taken me years to get over that loss, but even more stunning was the interview of the MVP Quarterback, Tom Brady, shortly after the Patriot victory.

"It's got to be amazing being on top of the world - the best QB in the league, another Super Bowl championship, several sponsorships, all the female fans, power, influence, etc.," the interviewer gushed.

What came next shocked and perplexed many football fans who were watching. Quite matter-of-factly, Tom Brady replied, "There's got to be more to life than this!"

"More to life than this?!" I thought. *Wow.*

This came from a man who supposedly "had it all." And yet, he didn't know his true reason for existing. Was his purpose simply to be the best football player in the league, or was it more than that?

One of the greatest Olympic swimmers of all time, Michael Phelps gave us another example of purpose to examine. Victory after victory, medal after medal, Phelps was simply unstoppable. He made history winning his 8th gold medal at the 2008 Beijing Olympics, but what happened shortly after is common among athletes who have attained their loftiest goals: He plunged into a deep depression. As with many accomplished and well-trained athletes, **his goal became his purpose**.

Let me be crystal clear: I'm absolutely in favor of setting and accomplishing goals. I actually help people do that. But there's a line that we must be careful not to cross. When a goal becomes our deepest mission, it can set us up for a huge letdown. We reach the goal only to realize that there is life after achievement, and then we're stumped as to why we're still here. Unsurprisingly, this can give rise to depression and apathy.

Purpose comes before goals and accomplishments, not the other way around. Purpose is not limited to positions, titles, responsibilities, and roles we play from day to day. Instead, our purpose is played out through whatever roles and activities we have daily. When I ask people what their purpose is, I often hear, "being a great dad" or "being the best mom I can be" or even "being a great example to my employees." This is admirable, but when we finish raising our kids, then what? What happens when our employees take other jobs or change careers? If the definition of our purpose - a major piece of our identity - is in some way dependent on the presence of others, we are missing the critical element of independence.

I've visited the Middle East a handful of times over the past 10 years to share my Inside Out Leadership program with leaders crossing into every sphere of society. It has been an amazing experience, as I always have far more to learn from them than they do from me. It's always refreshing to hear the top question I am asked when I set foot in that region of the world. What do you suppose they ask the most?

Many people assume it has to do with how tall I am (I'm 6'4" so I get that a lot), or what brings me over to that region, or whether I played professional basketball - but I'm rarely asked about what I *do*. Instead, it involves who I *am*. They ask, in so many words, "Who are you?" They essentially want to know what makes my heart beat faster - what make me come alive. The first time I was asked this question, I must be honest, I was floored and taken completely off guard!

If you were asked this question, how would you respond?

Who are you?

It's a fascinating and challenging query. It throws us off because in the Western world, we ask a very different question! What are you asked when you meet someone for the first time?

Yes, you guessed it! *"What do you do?"*

We are so accustomed to letting people know what we do that it can easily start to define who we are.

Thus, we experience an identity crisis. We shout our titles, positions, accomplishments, and accolades in everyday conversations by default. It's all we know. After all, it's all we've been taught. Meanwhile, we have lost who we really are. We operate from a position, a title; we wear that badge proudly. But when we have a rough day at work, guess what happens? We're down in the dumps, our self-worth plummets, and we strap ourselves in for an emotional rollercoaster. Surely I'm not the only one who has taken that ride. Other times, we land a big deal or achieve a big goal and our emotions skyrocket. Ultimately, we let what we do define who we are and suffer through the unpredictable ups and downs. What an opportunity we have in our self-discovery process to find out who we *actually* are!

Imagine you become stranded on a desert island for a full year. You have food, water, and all of life's bare necessities. However, you are stripped of every title and responsibility in your life. Nothing exists but you. How would you rate your self-worth on a scale from 1 to 10? 10 being, "Yeah! I enjoy who I am. I don't need anything or anyone," and 1 being, "I'm lost. My self-worth is completely diminished." Take a moment and honestly consider this. Would your sense of self-worth hold up?

Since the beginning of recorded history until now, researchers estimate that more than 100 billion people have lived on earth. (Can you imagine having to calculate these things?) Despite those numbers, there has never been, there is not, and there will never be anyone exactly like you. Even among the 7.5 billion people currently alive and the masses that will live in the future, you will always remain unique.

You love the way no one else loves, you solve problems in ways no one else does, you help people in ways no one else does, you think thoughts no one else thinks, and only you can fulfill your specific purpose!

If you want to discover (or re-discover) your purpose, the first step is to lower your guard and embrace who you are.

Over years of working with leaders around the world, I've uncovered 5 practical steps to help you discover who you are. Now, let's take a closer look at each step so you can unlock your purpose.

Unlock Your Purpose by Defining Core Values

What do you stand for?

This question can help us unearth our personal core values. Even though there are many facets of who you are, your core values are the steering wheel that guides your vehicle.

As an entrepreneur who has researched, observed, led, managed, trained, and coached highly influential people, I have come to learn that helping people discover their personal values is one of the ways I live a life of purpose. For example, one of my core values is commitment. I once heard someone say, "You are either in or out. There's no life in between." This concept stuck with me. It means everything to me that people can count on my word, and I also hold others accountable for their word. It's crucial that I know this about myself, and others need to know this about me too. If not, I might place unhealthy expectations on others if they fail to meet my standard of commitment. Knowing our core values helps us avoid being judgmental toward those that value different things.

Identifying and naming your values helps you comprehend the motives behind your decisions. As a result of this understanding, you maximize your potential as a person and as a leader.

A great resource to help you discover these core values in yourself is John Maxwell's Leadership Values Cards.

You can only meet your own expectations if you know your values. Furthermore, by knowing what your team members value, you can touch their hearts and become the leader they want. The Values Cards will start you down the path of understanding relational and values-based leadership.

Your core values are the strong convictions of your heart. They dictate what matters to you! As a matter of fact, you are making decisions from this core place every day, but you may not realize it. Our values affect our choices, how we solve problems, our priorities, our behavior in certain situations, and even how we treat people...Wow!

It has been hotly debated whether we are born with these convictions or if they are a learned behavior. What do you think? I like to think it's a little of both. (Go figure. I've always been a peacemaker!) On one hand, I know people that seem to have never wavered or questioned their set of values. On the other hand, I know people who appeared to have a strong value that was learned from their parents, only to grow up and exchange that value for another. Interesting, right? Nevertheless, whether you are born with them or they shift over time, core values anchor us in meaning.

Discover Your Strengths

"It's more important to improve your weaknesses than your strengths!"

Through the years, I have heard this sentiment echoed by a lot of people. The belief is that when you focus on developing weak areas, they begin to catch up with your strengths. But what would happen if we instead started nurturing the strengths we have been given?

Benjamin Franklin once said, "Hide not your talents. They for use were made. What's a sundial in the shade?"

I am all about improving weaknesses, but we have to be careful where the majority of our attention goes. Think about it. Strengths typically give way to enthusiasm, confidence, energy, and purpose, whereas weaknesses typically yield more frustration, discouragement, and disappointment. In addition, we tend to engage in our strengths effortlessly and our weaknesses with great striving. So in what direction should we aim more focus?

If you spend more time on strengths, you are more focused on who you are and less focused on who you should be. In *Strengths Finder 2.0*, Tom Rath says:

"At its fundamentally flawed core, the aim of almost any learning program is to help us become who we are not. If you don't have natural talent with numbers, you're still forced to spend time in that area to attain a degree. If you're not very empathic, you get sent to a course designed to infuse empathy into your personality. From cradle to cubical, we devote more time to our shortcoming than to our strengths."

Earlier, I shared how as a young entrepreneur it was easy for me to compare myself with other successful business people.

If only I had their intelligence, education, connections, finances, or creative ideas, then I'd be on my way!

I placed my focus on what I didn't have, and to be honest, it led to more and more striving. I was trying to become someone I wasn't. But as I learned to embrace my strengths, my life purpose unraveled and I was shown how I can best serve my family, business, and community.

Finding Passion Leads to Impact

After co-founding a non-denominational community church years ago, I began feeling the pull to do it again just a few years later. So I obeyed God's call to bring forth another church, but this time it was a simple community that would later become Meeting House Ministries. I told you I was a serial entrepreneur!

My passion became more evident to others as I invited them into a simpler way of life. The more I committed my time to being present with, loving, and serving each individual person, the surer I became that it was a lifestyle anyone could access. As a natural result, it began to rub off on others - that's what passion does!

More than 8 years later, Meeting House Ministries has become a worldwide network that is passionate about building healthy, spiritual communities. Our life together is expressed in 3 spheres: Upward through thanksgiving, worship and prayer; Inward through testimony, training, equipping, and meals; and Outward through local and global service. Talk about passion!

When you are driven by passion, people see it in your eyes, hear it in your voice, experience it in your body language, and sense it in the atmosphere. **Passion is contagious.**

People want to be around those who are passionate. They want to buy from passionate people, partner with passionate people, work for passionate people, and be led by passionate people.

Here are 3 practical questions to ask yourself:

1. Am I spending the majority of my time on things I'm passionate about?
2. What should I do with my life *now*?
3. What's one step I can take toward one of my passions?

Your business can't succeed without passion. Answering these questions will aid you in realizing where your passion lies.

Milestones Reveal Your Purpose

mile-stone (n.)
1. An important event, as in a person's career, the history of a nation, or the advancement of knowledge in a field; a turning point.

Rose F. Kennedy once said, "Life isn't a matter of milestones but of moments."

We all have moments that shaped us into the people we are today. These life-changing events can be interpreted as both good and bad.

No one is completely removed from the most amazing and challenging things life has to offer.

We don't always fully grasp the impact milestones have until we look back on them weeks, months, or years later. Life milestones are the significant moments where we, knowingly or unknowingly, put a stake in the ground where we never have before. Our lives are never quite the same afterwards.

For me, one of those life milestones was the day I asked my wife Karen to marry me. Of course, our wedding day was spectacular on its own, but there was something distinctly special about the day I asked for her hand in marriage.

I am a strategic planner, so I had carefully conceived of the perfect day to pop the question! However, things didn't go as planned.

I awoke one morning, going through my usual prayer and gratitude time with God. And although it was a month ahead of schedule, I felt a strong tug on my heart that morning. I knew it was the day to ask Karen to marry me.

Now for a planner like me, this threw me for a big loop! I got to work, arranging all of the moving parts in a very short period of time. I thank God that He helped me get things in order, and I accomplished a month's worth of planning in less than 12 hours.

I invited Karen out to a beautiful lake not far from our homes, leading her beside the sandy edge of the water. I was as nervous as they come, but I didn't let her see me sweat. At least... I didn't think so.

Silently, I began to pray for our relationship, which was not uncommon. But on that day, mid-prayer, I dropped to one knee and nervously began my proposal. As I took the ring out of my pocket, it slipped between my fingers. Everything appeared to be in slow motion as I fumbled to catch it, unsuccessfully, and watched it land silently on the sandy ground. Briskly, I picked it up, blew off the sand, and we continued our engagement as we laughed.

Looking back on it now, I am still reminded of what this funny and awkward time represented in my life. It was a milestone in which I overcame a major trust hurdle that I struggled with since high school. As you can imagine, being a sensitive kid and learning of my parents' divorce wasn't easy. I didn't know if I could ever sincerely trust another human being again, let alone for the rest of my life. This is why milestones are so important. They challenge us, change us, and permanently alter the trajectory of our lives. Of course, Karen and I experience challenges, but our marriage is vibrant and healthy to say the least! I am forever thankful for this milestone that dramatically changed my perspective on life.

Exercise: Analyze Your Milestones

Life milestones help you unveil your life purpose. Think through the different periods of your life. Begin with the early years and move through each stage, completing the exercise in bite-sized pieces (for example: early childhood, adolescent, college-age, young professional, early marriage, starting a family, etc.).

As you go through each period, ask yourself, "What life-changing moments occurred in this period that molded me into the person I am today?" Pinpoint your life-changing moments - things that were wonderful, difficult, painful, or extraordinary.

Once you have these milestones selected, contemplate the impact that each milestone had on you. What are the meanings you attach to these past experiences?

Examining these events gives you a clearer view of your life purpose.

Discover Your Gift by Knowing Your Temperament

Everyone has been given useful gifts, with one primary gift bestowed upon each of us the moment we are conceived. Psychologists group us into "basic temperaments" or personality types, which help us distinguish our gifts from someone else's.

When we identify and accept these powerful gifts, amazing transformation occurs in the world. These gifts are not only meant for you, but for others to benefit from too. Your gifts are an integral part of the broader picture. As we learn to operate within our gifts, we leave a legacy of goodness behind for generations to come. How exciting!

I have come to realize that my primary gift is to encourage others. It is my joy to be a conduit for encouragement and inspiration to people all over the world. I am humbled to see things in people that they are unable to see in themselves. Something comes alive in me when I meet someone who is down and I can help lift them into a higher perspective.

Are you ready to find out your primary gift?

The first step is to identify your dominant temperament. There are several ways to get to know yourself better in this arena. Luckily, psychology has a plethora of resources, like the Myers Briggs personality test or the DISC assessment. (Temperament resources like these can be found at www.leadthewaybook.com/jointhemovement). These tests will give you deep insight into your levels of introversion/extroversion, reveal how you make decisions (e.g. head or heart), and explain how you cognitively process your experiences. Knowing your temperament will help you navigate the professional world and get acquainted with your strengths and weaknesses.

The next step is to accept your gifts, be thankful, and never take them for granted. Of course, accepting your gifts isn't always easy. As we discussed back in Chapter 4, comparison thoughts can creep into your mind. If you find yourself comparing your gifts with the gifts of others, you are striving to be someone else. Remember: When we do this, we stop embracing who we are!

Once you have accepted your gift, cherish it, appreciate it, and cultivate it with confidence and sensitivity. This is your essential driver.

It is your gift, and no one can take it from you. When you become aware of the temperament in you, it becomes easier to cultivate an Inside Out perspective.

Life Celebration Exercise: Summarize Who You Are

Have you ever attended a memorial service? Who would come to your service? Who would give the eulogy and what would they say?

You may be saying, "Yikes. So much for being positive!" But bear with me! To live intentionally, we have to come to terms with the end of life. So from this perspective, here is your chance to be in charge. YOU get to choose what is said at your own service.

Let's take a look back at the 5 key areas that helped you discover who you are. These will help you construct your eulogy intentionally. Have fun with this exercise!

- **Core Values:** What is important to you?
- **Strengths:** Distinct abilities
- **Life Milestones**: Unique things in life that shaped you
- **Passions:** What to devote your life to!
- **Gifts**: What you leave to the world

We have come here to celebrate and honor the life of _____.
He/She brought (Core Values) _____
_____to the world by His/Her
(Strengths) _____
_____ through His/Her (Life Milestones) _____
_____

_____
and committed to (Passions) _____
and ultimately gave the legacy of (Gifts) _____
_____.

Reflection: WHY Am I Really Here?

When you understand and embrace who you are, the next appropriate question to ask is, "Why do I exist?" You now have your gifts, knowledge, and new resources at your disposal. How do they feed into and assist with your purpose?

Defining your purpose isn't so much about having all the language down pat so you can frame it and hang it on a wall. True purpose is extremely difficult to define because it is so deep, so strong, and so compelling that words cannot adequately describe it. However, I'll do my best to help you get some of it on paper!

Practical Steps

1. What specific problem in the world compels you to rise up and say, "This will not happen as long as I'm alive!" This issue makes you come alive, stand up, and be a voice for others that may not feel that they have one.
2. How can I actively become a solution to this problem?

CHAPTER 7

Develop an Attitude of Gratitude

"Enjoy the little things, for one day you may look back and realize they were the big things." - Robert Brault

ANOTHER CORE CONVICTION OF Inside Out leaders is that they have learned the importance of gratitude. Some might call it a perspective of abundance! It doesn't matter what challenging situations arise. They just find the flame of hope, fan it, and watch it grow larger. Then, they begin to rally other people around the fire. Those who operate from gratitude are not held back by adversity, obstacles, circumstances, etc. They see difficulties as opportunities for growth and invite others into the growth process.

The World's Current of Negativity

Everywhere we turn, we are hit with waves of negativity without even realizing it. Turn on the news, what do you hear? A vast majority of the time, news outlets cover the bad far more often than the good - a shooting, a kidnapping, a bomb threat, a missing child, stock markets at an all-time low. It is sometimes important to report negative events, but we hear far too little about the plethora of positive things happening. Even when good news is reported, it is pushed into a small section of a news website or covered in one evening news segment - certainly not repeated night after night like the bad news is.

Imagine what would happen if people gained a more upbeat perspective on life. How might the world look different?

One beautiful afternoon not too long ago, I was taking a walk around our neighborhood with my kids. It was 75 degrees and sunny with a slight breeze blowing. Along our travels, I happened to run into a neighbor.

I said, "Man, isn't this an amazing day!?"

The neighbor responded, "Yeah, but it's not going to be here for long. It's going to storm in a few days."

I couldn't believe how easily he bypassed the positive to talk about a potential negative that hadn't even happened yet!

We have to realize what we are up against to make a sustained positive change. It starts as soon as we wake up in the morning. We are bombarded with negativity. Our own thought patterns start to have a negative slant. Our minds quickly start racing about the tough phone call we have to make or the difficult conversation we need to have.

Consider how Monday morning goes for most people. I know many leaders that say, "This is going to be a long week."

My response is always the same. "Keep telling yourself that, and that's what it will be." It's called a self-fulfilling prophecy. I love self-fulfilled prophecies, but mostly when the impact is positive.

We become what we believe.

I'll say it once more: We become what we believe. We have talked about the negative news and our own negative thought patterns, but what about social media? If someone doesn't like our Facebook post, it shouldn't leave us down in the dumps (not to mention the political crossfire on social media that has torn apart friendships and families).

Let's have some fun for a minute. (If I don't, I might start to fall into this negativity stuff. Ha!) In America, we have one intentional day for giving thanks: Thanksgiving Day. However, families can get real negative real fast around the dinner table. It's astonishing. Pay attention the next time you're at a Thanksgiving meal. One negative or sarcastic comment turns into two and the next thing you know, the entire meal is hijacked by a current of negativity.

Inside Out leaders don't give in and let the world dictate their perspective on people, situations, and problems. They have an attitude of gratitude, and they're very intentional about practicing it so they can build a lifestyle out of thankfulness. These Inside Out leaders transform their environment rather than being transformed by it. In the midst of negativity, they offer hope, anticipation, and expectancy, regardless of how difficult a situation appears on the surface.

I'm reminded of a time my niece called me up and said, "Uncle Robb, I have a project in one of my classes. I'm supposed to find a family member or a close friend that has a life quote that they live by, and I knew I could call you. You always have a lot to say. So, Uncle Robb, what's a life quote that you live by that you came up with on your own?"

My response was, **"Much of the world either sees the glass half empty or half filled, but I always see it overflowing."**

Remember our perspective discussion in Chapter 1? If you can see the hope, if you can see the light in every situation, whether it's a good day or a bad day, you are focused on life. When you're focused on life, you become a witness, noticing more and more light that is flowing around you. As leaders, we are change agents. We change environments and we have the power to change dynamics from negative to positive. That's a very significant power.

Every day, I make a choice. I begin each day with an intentional time of gratitude. I call this the "first fruits" principle. I am committed to giving God my undivided attention as soon as I wake up. As soon as I open my eyes, I think of a few things for which I am grateful. Many times, I will take a deep breath and gives thanks that I'm alive, He is alive, I have health, I have family, I'm going to meet new people today, etc. Then I head downstairs, grab my cup of coffee, and continue my gratitude party. During this time, I think through more specific aspects of my life for which I am grateful. It can be as simple as the tires on my car having air or how a specific person is patient with me. It's not unlike me to also pick up the bible and read some encouraging stories and apply them to my life.

I love to get up early and spend time alone giving thanks. But it's even more fun as my family members trickle downstairs and join in. We speak, act out, or draw the things for which we are thankful. After a few minutes together, I will close with a thankful prayer and we get going for the day.

Now, I know what you're probably thinking.

"...Do you work!?"

To be honest, some mornings it lasts 10 minutes and others it extends to an hour, depending on our schedules. The temptations are there for me, as they are for all of us - turn on the TV, check work messages, check social media. I've just decided that I'm not going to begin my day that way. We have made a commitment to God and one another that we will give Him our "first fruits" at the beginning of each day. It has helped us gain a much higher perspective on life while redefining success individually and collectively.

Gratitude Is a Muscle

With the constant stream of negativity that surrounds us, we have to work out our gratitude muscle each day. Think of the discipline that is required when someone wants to lose weight. Gratitude is no different.

When we stay committed to working out our gratitude muscle day in and day out, it becomes bigger, stronger, and others can't help but notice the difference! **Once gratitude takes root in our hearts, it becomes who we are as opposed to something we do.**

Gratitude - A Look Ahead

A friend of mine once shared with me a purposeful way he approaches each new year. It's a powerful way to tackle each day too: A look back, a look up, and a look ahead. A look back is a time of thankful reflection. A look up is a time of thankful perspective. A look ahead is a time of thankful future.

It's one thing to be thankful for what has already happened, but we can also be thankful for what's to come! The past has already taken place, so it's easier to reflect on these tangible things. **However, when we rejoice in what has not yet happened, we begin to operate from faith.** Faith believes in what you hope for and is certain of what you do not see. We are either operating out of faith or fear. There is really no in-between.

If you can gratefully look upon the things that haven't actually happened yet, anticipation grows in your day-to-day life. It's as if you are venturing out on an Easter egg hunt every day. There are nuggets of hidden treasure for you to find. This practice enables us to tap into the child within; it's playful, it's adventurous, and it builds strong positive momentum!

There are new people to meet, new things to do, new problems to solve, new possibilities to pursue, and new doors to open! When our heart is open to gratitude for what's to come, we go about life keeping an eye out for those things. In other words, we condition ourselves to look for the good.

Gratitude in All Things

Intentional times of gratitude give way to living a lifestyle of gratitude.
When there is gratefulness in all things, what can possibly hold us back? This mindset of abundance begins to break through the levies in our hearts and minds.

Now I know you might be thinking, "Seriously...in *all* things? I'm human. I'm going to get hurt. I'm going to be hit with curveballs in life."

Remember, we don't have to like what we're going through. However, we can ask: Can I see any life in the midst of the pain, the hurt, the challenge? I encourage you to look for the little bit of light even in your deepest, darkest moments. When we focus on that little spark, it ignites and fosters the thankful spirit. Before long, the spark catches fire and draws others closer to it!

A Surprising Way to Increase Productivity

If your business relied on your emotional stability for its success, how long would you actually be in business? Humans experience a wide spectrum of emotions depending on the situation. It often sidelines our productivity, but does it *always* have to be like that? One of the keys to living an emotionally controlled life is thankfulness.

You might be thinking, "If you only knew my situation! There's not a whole lot to be thankful for."

A few years ago at work, it seemed like everything that could go wrong went wrong for me. I was putting out fire after fire, all day long. It just kept getting worse.

At that time, I was the president of a basketball clothing company during the day and the director of a motivational basketball camp at night. After a particularly rough day, I got into my car and drove 15 minutes across town to run motivational basketball clinics for 30 energetic 5 to 7-year-olds. I was normally excited to be with the kids, but this day was different.

As I wallowed in my problems, I realized that I had the choice to continue on this downward spiral or choose to be thankful. I was determined to be thankful even though my body was revolting against it. From that willful determination, I started listing all the people and things for which I was grateful. To my surprise, it got easier the more I did it. After a few minutes, I started feeling a little better. By the time I arrived at the clinic, I had an abundance of energy, focus, and joy.

When you choose to be thankful, you live a more consistent life of balanced emotions, which leads to consistent productivity.

As I'm writing this, I can't help myself…

- I am grateful for the opportunity to write this book!
- I am grateful for my wife and 3 children!
- I am grateful for my personal relationship with Jesus Christ!
- I am grateful for my specific purpose!
- I am grateful for my good health!
- I am grateful for mentors in my life!
- I am grateful for my entire biological and spiritual family!
- I am grateful for my house, neighborhood, and friends!
- I am grateful to be alive during this time in human history!
- I am grateful for my amazing team at Holman International!

Practical Step: What are you are thankful for right now? Be specific.

CHAPTER 8

Find Power in Personal Vision

"The only thing worse than being blind is having sight but no vision." -Helen Keller

ON MY MOM'S 50ᵀᴴ birthday, she wanted to fulfill her lifelong dream of flying in a hot air balloon. One problem: I was terrified of heights! In addition, I was on medication for high blood pressure. But I was so grateful for the lifetime of love and support my mom had poured out for me, I knew I had to do it for her. It was a small token of appreciation for all the years she helped shape me. I just had to figure out how in the world I would face this monstrous fear.

The balloon basket was only as high as my waist (remember, I'm a 6' 4" ex-basketball player). Every time they fired the burner to take us higher, I was convinced my eyebrows would be singed off. To say I was anxious would be a massive understatement. As our balloon gently lifted off the ground, I could feel the stress rising in every part of me. Every muscle in me tensed, but I wouldn't let my mom see it. I just couldn't rob her of the joy of the experience. As we gradually floated higher,

I prepared myself to totally collapse in fear. But instead, something strange and completely unexpected happened.

The negative feelings began to subside. Tension, anxiety, and terror were gradually replaced by peace, joy, excitement, anticipation- even freedom!

As we reached our maximum altitude, I saw a different view of my surroundings. I began to relax and even enjoy the journey. Before long, I found myself reflecting on what I was capable of from a place of strength I didn't know I had — all with my mother by my side.

When you courageously face your fears and let go of control, it is possible to reach unimaginable heights and see from a totally different perspective. You can finally see the whole picture (in this example, quite literally!). I felt bigger in the balloon, while everything else felt smaller. I felt as though I could do anything. From this place, vision comes alive.

Thank you, mom.

Vision Uncovered

Vision is SO overused in business settings that we've pretty much forgotten what it really means and how it affects us. Vision is such a powerful fuel for inspiration that it compels us to reclaim it. When you think "vision," what immediately comes to mind? Mission, dreams, destiny, big picture, change, identity, purpose, future?

Vision is the use of our imagination to experientially see into a preferred future state. Once this future state has been conceived, it can start to take root in our reality. In other words, it becomes so tangible, it's as though it already happened.

I'm reminded of some transformational leaders in human history who functioned quite powerfully from their own personal vision. They saw into the future so profoundly that their visions helped future generations evolve. You can probably already think of some of these people by name.

Their visions were so developed that they laid down their life for it - faith martyrs, presidents, civil rights leaders, philanthropists, etc. What about business leaders?

If you've ever seen the famous TED Talk, How to Find Work You Love, you may remember Scott Dinsmore. Scott began his career in a lucrative position with a Fortune 500 company, but soon found that he hated it. "At about 10 a.m. every morning I had this strange urge to slam my head through the monitor of the computer," he quipped.

Soon after this realization, Scott took a leap and founded Live Your Legend, a company that assists people in finding and succeeding in work they love. As an entrepreneur and avid adventurer, Scott walked the walk, doing the work he "couldn't not do" - travelling the world, making friends everywhere he went, and leading by example. This led him to Mount Kilimanjaro, where an accident took his life at age 33. His death was seen as a devastating tragedy by the countless people he inspired, but in Scott's mind, the real tragedy would have been if he had skipped that fateful trip. A week before his death he wrote, "To pass up an adventure I've talked about for years because I couldn't find the courage to do it? That would have been a tragedy." Today, Scott's message is spreading faster and echoing louder than ever with the help of his wife, friends, and colleagues who continue to run Live Your Legend.

Leaders like Jesus of Nazareth, Martin Luther King, Jr., Gandhi, and many others could see years beyond their present time. With passion, conviction, and boldness, they pulled ideas from that future state and never stopped pulling. **They pulled on this future state until it started to break into the present.** One of the amazing things about these leaders is that many gave their life for the cause before they could see it all play out. The ripple effect that occurred when they gave their lives continues to reach generations beyond. It continues to radiate outward today, and it will still be radiating tomorrow.

Do you have a vision worth dying for? There is an old saying, "Without vision, the people perish." I find this to be true. Little by little, people shrivel up on the inside and become the walking dead without a personal vision. But there's always another way.

Many business owners and leaders envision big things, but is their vision so personal and so powerful that they'd be willing to die for it?

I know what you're thinking. "Come on Robb, like I'd really die just for a business vision!" **But remember that Inside Out leadership is about living from such a strong personal vision that it bleeds right into your business! When you are willing to die for your vision, you are ready to start living for it now!** Let's take a closer look at the 3 main areas that will ramp up the power of your personal vision.

Purpose is the foundation from which we dream!

We can dream all day long and have grand ideas, but it's the purpose underneath that keeps a vision alive! I personally believe that so many visions are cut short because people don't realize *why* they're here. They lack a purposeful foundation that answers "who am I?" and "why am I here?"

A purposeful foundation is critical because it's the stable place from which you envision. When you are rooted in personal purpose, your dreams run deep. Far from unrealistic, they're anchored by meaning and significance.

When you come to terms with your purpose (as we discussed in Chapter 6), vision transforms from something that looks and sounds good to something that's deep, sustainable, and reproducible.

Have you ever had a major wake-up call? The most amazing possibilities and opportunities come about in the aftermath of wake-up calls.

For me, one of my big wake-up calls (and God knows I've had many of them) was in high school when I was forced to face my parents' divorce. As a sensitive and highly relational high school graduate, I continued my journey at Widener University, a small college right outside of Philadelphia, Pennsylvania. I was in so much emotional and spiritual pain that for my first 3 years I would take late night walks around campus and find some quiet, dark places to cry and get my emotions out.

Why is this happening to me? Why can't things be different?

Fast forward to the summer before my senior year. I was 21 and about ready to embark on the best year of my life. At least, that's what I thought - senior year, business student, captain of a national NCAA basketball team. People assumed I was on top of the world.

Secretly, I had been rocked with some bad news. I had a mass in my midsection that went undiagnosed for nearly a month and a half. I missed most of the pre-season basketball training and was still struggling heavily with my parents' divorce and other problems. It was like everything came to a head. Remember back in Chapter 5 (Lead Yourself First) when we discussed the importance of spirit, soul, and body? Well, my emotions were overwhelmed by my parents' divorce, my body was obviously breaking down, and I was questioning my spiritual life because God felt so distant. Hurt and confused, I shut down.

I've got to be honest with you. Leading up to this point, purpose for me was drinking with friends on the weekends and winning the next basketball game. That's what got me out of bed in the morning. But after being hit with my diagnosis, I began asking questions that I'd never asked before.

What does my life even mean?

Doctors feared that the mass was cancerous. It was so unusual that the medical specialists had never seen anything like it. I was given scan after scan, MRI after MRI, and multiple ultrasounds. The "best of the best" specialists didn't know what it was, and even worse, they didn't know how to treat it!

I have cancer, and I'm going to die.

The thought kept running through my head. Like many people who are faced with the unknown, I came to grips with the worst case scenario.

Finally, someone suggested I meet with an ultrasound specialist who I had not yet seen at the University of Pennsylvania Hospital. As he examined me, he couldn't believe what he saw.

"I can't explain it, but what you had coming in, you don't have any longer."

I was dumbfounded and taken back. *Did I hear him correctly?*

He said, "Look. I'm going to show you on the ultrasound screen, so pay close attention."

At that moment I perked up and my eyes locked onto the screen. We both scanned the screen up and down, left and right, but saw absolutely nothing. The mass was gone.

It was a modern day miracle that radically altered my perspective. The best way I can describe the feeling was like spiritual fireworks going off in the depths of my being. Immediately, purpose went from winning the next basketball game to "I'm alive for a reason, and I gotta find out what that reason is!"

Though I didn't know precisely what my purpose was, I knew that a foundation of purpose was being built and that I'd be changed forever!

What has happened in your life - good or bad - that has awakened you? What are some questions that arose since that poignant experience?

It's experiences like these that bring us to a crossroad: Allow yourself to be buried in self-pity, burden, and struggle, or allow yourself to evolve. Let the challenge pierce deep. Walking out of the doctor's office that day, I got curious.

Wow. I do have significance. I'm going to find out why I'm here and what I can do to have a truly unique impact.

Take a Vision Trip

A vision trip is an exploratory, short-term trip taken with people who share a similar, purpose-driven vision. These journeys allow us to collect important information on a topic that interests us, while engaging in strategic conversations with others involved. Typically, vision trips provide a renewed vision of hope, a sense of community, and experiential understanding of what a future state could look like for you.

10 years after my miraculous healing experience in college, I heard about some extraordinary work being done in the Middle East - stories

of wonderful people doing amazing humanitarian and leadership work. By this time, I had already started a few non-profit and for-profit organizations and was pretty well-networked. Not to mention, I was energized by the idea of using my leadership gift to serve people in a region where very few were willing to go. So the more I researched, the more compelled I felt to take this trip with a good friend.

Imagine being married 3 years and telling your spouse that you feel strongly pulled to take a vision trip into one of the most volatile regions of the world. You better believe that a lot of contemplation and deep conversation went into this decision. In the end, my wife and I believed (despite much opposition and concern from close family and friends) that I needed to take this very timely trip.

As my friend and I prepared for the journey, ideas were bubbling up about what we could potentially do. I knew we needed to experience it with our own eyes and ears.

I wondered if this could be a region of the world that we served in the long-term - a place where we could meet the practical needs of current leaders, while inspiring and positively influencing the leaders of tomorrow. There was only one way to find out - go!

When we arrived in Afghanistan, I was not quite prepared for everything we saw. We first assisted an organization that served orphan children. These children wandered the streets, surviving off of food found in trashcans. Many of them lived in what are referred to as "tent communities," which have little to no life necessities. Through the organization, the children received help getting washed and were given some fun, interactive games to play. In addition to helping with this, I was able to use my basketball background to help train a local basketball team. It was a profound opportunity to use our skillsets in business, leadership, and basketball to facilitate the first official high school basketball tournament in the school and city history. Pretty awesome!

During our 14-day vision trip, my personal vision became clearer, but not at all how I expected. After these eye-opening experiences, ideas flooded my mind and a lot of discussions came up.

"This really interests me. This is a really passionate area for me. Maybe we should pursue this, maybe that? I'm not really sure. What do you think?"

For us, the vision trip took our purpose and really stirred the pot. An interactive idea-sifting process began. In time, I became laser focused on my personal vision and ended up going back to the Middle East 4 times in a span of 8 years. I brought with me teams of people who were ready to assist and impact leaders in various spheres of society.

As a result of my vision trip, I realized I had to use my leadership gift and become a catalyst for my network to make a long-term impact. For this to happen, I willingly surrendered some other local and regional opportunities as my personal vision came into focus. The trip granted me the chance to sift through what I needed to sift through. I gained clarity in areas I otherwise wouldn't have. Ideas became more structured and tangible as I talked and listened to others who were further along in the process. I found words for what I was feeling because I saw with my own eyes, felt with my own body, and experienced what I hadn't before.

What would your vision trip look like? Maybe you don't go to the Middle East. Maybe it's simply the east side of town. As your purpose ignites, it will lead you to new locations where you can progress. You may interview pioneers, learn from mentors, and engage with people who have already worked in your passion areas. The specifics are up to you – but it all starts with you envisioning it.

Crafting Your Vision

It is imperative to engage ALL of your senses in the dreaming process. You want to hear, see, smell, taste, and feel your preferred future state. So many dreams are cut short because people only vaguely engage with them. This is a surefire way to keep your dreams and your reality separate.

The greatest leaders in human history fully envisioned life 20 years down the line. They were experiencing the future in the present. They saw it, tasted it, smelled it, touched it, and felt it. It was so alive for them that it was only a matter of time before it became a reality.

My friend and I returned home from our vision trip and talked about how our plans were becoming more real. It felt good to recuperate and gain more knowledge in hindsight of the trip. At that point, we knew we needed to recalibrate and spend some time envisioning. Branching off on our own, we went to be silent, to pray, and to think through our plans, engaging all of our senses.

Here is a common example of how this dream process works. An expecting mother or father will think about their child well before their physical arrival. They wonder what their child will look and sound like, and what it will feel like the first time they hold them. Nothing has occurred, yet in anticipation, parents vividly imagine and engage all of their senses as though the baby was already born.

Personal vision works just the same. Be still. Be quiet. Consider your purpose and fast forward your life to the positive things that will happen as a result. Spend some time and camp out in this vision. Go through your sensory perceptions and write down what you experience. Be as specific as possible. You will see yourself achieving far more than you could ever come up with on the spot. It's as though you are tapping into foresight.

You have an opportunity. No matter what curveball life throws at you, no matter what has rocked your boat beyond comprehension, you have an opportunity to be awakened. When you awaken, there's no telling what can happen because that awakening draws us to have internal conversations we'd never have otherwise.

In the midst of all this, I want to encourage you to take some alone time. For some of you this may include quiet music in the background. For others it could simply mean taking a walk in nature. Regardless of how you do it, find space to be alone. Engage your senses. Just watch and see what develops!

Practical Step: Start Dreaming!

If you knew you couldn't fail, what would you spend your time on? What would you do? What would you be? Write down your actions and their outcomes. Be specific and engage all 5 senses. Here are the parameters:

1. Make it like a Christmas list!
2. No time limit (could be 1, 5, or 20 years)
3. Let your mind run free - keep the pen moving.
4. Consider all aspects of your life. (Emotional, physical, career, family, financial, spiritual, etc.)

CHAPTER 9

Create a Plan of Action

"Unless commitment is made, there are only promises and hopes; but no plans." - Peter F. Drucker

HAVE YOU EVER BEEN excited about a vacation to somewhere you've never been? You've done all the internet research, talked to family and friends, created a schedule of fun activities, mapped out your course of action, and even started packing days in advance. There's something blissful about getting away for pure enjoyment! The only thing that could ruined such a trip would be getting lost - not being able to find your destination.

Even in the age of the internet, we sometimes get lost. A destination is nothing without a GPS guiding you. **In life, our vision is the destination, and our action plan is the GPS**. We can have all the visions in the world, but if we don't create and implement a plan, we set ourselves up to fail. Action plans are the roadmap to vision success!

Give Your Vision an Action Plan

I have been working out at my local YMCA for years. Year after year, I can't help but notice the influx of people that pour in immediately following New Year's Day. Of course, I love the heart many people have after a new year begins. However, I've observed a down-hill trend (and I'm sure I'm not alone) in which the vast majority of those spirited people drop off after the first 2 weeks. Nearly all of them are gone within 45 days. The bright side is that at least a remnant of them stick around. Statistics say that approximately 6% of people stay the course. Just 6 out of 100! I don't know about you, but I think there's something we can learn from those 6 individuals.

I love the Fast Company article by Gwen Moran, "5 Steps to Follow Through on Everything." In this, she captures the approach of motivation expert, Steve Levinson:

"1. BE HONEST ABOUT WHAT YOU WANT

Successful follow-through requires some up-front prep, including understanding what the true goal is. You might say that you want to get a promotion by the end of the year or hit your sales numbers out of the park, but why?

2. UNDERSTAND THE SACRIFICE

Every act takes away time or effort that could be committed to something else, Levinson says. Are you ready to make the trade-off? If your goal is to be more organized, you're going to need to spend time every day maintaining the system you put in place. Sales increases require more time prospecting and calling clients. Writing that book means planting your butt in the chair every day and actually writing. **Make sure you don't set yourself up for failure by creating demands that conflict with other priorities.**

3. PREPARE FOR SUCCESS

"Just do it" doesn't cut it, Levinson says. Invest a little time and maybe some money into your future success. If you're committed to following through on more leads, set up a system to capture the prospect's information and make it easy to follow up at regular intervals.

Create systems for as many of your goal-related tasks as possible. For example, use your accounting or customer relationship management system to follow up with 20 of your prospects every Monday morning. In some cases, you'll need to bring in other people or delegate some responsibilities so you can focus on what you need to get done, Levinson says.

Whatever your goal is, looking at the steps you'll need to take and enlisting the tools and people you'll need to help you get it done is a far more effective strategy than relying on sheer willpower.

"Willpower is both a precious commodity and an unreliable one. You really can't count on it. It often does not come through for you when you need it the most and the best thing to do is structure circumstances so that you don't need to rely on it," Levinson says.

4. GIVE YOURSELF DEADLINES

You know this, but it bears repeating: ***Break down the steps and assign a deadline to each.*** *It's the quickest way to tell at a glance if you're on track with your follow-through or not, Levinson says.*

5. INCENTIVIZE YOURSELF

As you're in the process of following through, use incentives and motivators to give you the kind of motivation you need when you need it. Levinson says his favorite story of the carrot and stick is that of a guy who wanted to go to the gym more often, so he left his one stick of deodorant there. If he didn't get up and go exercise in the morning, he was going to forego deodorant all day. *Maybe that's not realistic in the business world, but you can find ways to reward yourself when you hit follow-through milestones – dinner out with friends or a coveted purchase.* **Enlist friends or colleagues to help keep you accountable to the promises you make to yourself and others with regard to follow-through.**"

Accountability in Community

I must reinforce Levinson's suggestion to enlist friends and colleagues to help keep you accountable. Accountability promotes momentum in your life; it is a prized possession.

The healthiest form of accountability is found in a like-minded and purposeful community. When you surround yourself with others that have a similar heart, passion, and purpose, that are not afraid to call you to a higher way of life, finding accountability is easier.

As you continue on your Inside Out Leadership journey, it will be important for you to engage with others that are on a similar journey to help inspire your self-discovery process!

I've been so encouraged by our Lead the Way movement, which provides that source of encouragement and accountability for leaders around the world. We are committed to help serve and surround you with as many resources as we can to align your personal purpose with your professional work. (At the end of this book, you will be given a protected password to officially become a part of the Lead the Way movement and begin receiving additional resources to make sure you are not alone!)

People Die without Vision, Equally Die Without a Plan

Remember the saying, "Where there is no vision, the people perish?" Equally, I believe that people perish without a plan. A sustainable action plan is what carries your vision forth. It's an interesting dichotomy where passion meets process. You breathe life into an excel spreadsheet—a place where vibrancy marries long-term accountability.

In 2008, I founded a highly influential small business coaching company called Business Vision Network (BVN). BVN's passion was serving business owners and leaders by helping them build strong Inside Out Leadership™ foundations. Over the course of 8 years, we saw countless leaders literally change from the inside out through my leadership process. However, a problem became evident to me during this process: We lacked operational development tools and resources to help them sustain the Inside Out foundations they built. BVN helped business owners with some operational development, but our focus was primarily in the core Inside Out process.

In stepped Agents of Efficiency (AoE)!

Early in 2016, through a mutual friend, I met AoE, a company that is revolutionizing the way small businesses operate through its Efficiency Roadmap™ process. Justin E. Crawford founded AoE and is the chief architect of the Roadmap, a unique step-by-step process for helping small businesses thrive. He has written a best-selling book on his Roadmap process called *Live Free or DIY* (www.livefreebook.com). It's an ultra-practical guide that frees small business owners from the do-it-yourself trap that so often exhausts us. Justin's process helps unleash the kind of explosive growth many of us only dream about.

When I came across Agents of Efficiency, a light bulb went on in my mind. I started dreaming of what we could accomplish with the heart and soul of my company with the help of Justin's expertise. **BVN had the passion and AoE had the process.** It wasn't long after we met that we discovered we'd be even better working in partnership, learning from each other as each company grew.

There are 2 things that I want to illuminate in light of my story:

1. We had 1 side of the coin (Purpose, Passion, Vision) and AoE had the other side (Process, Plan).
2. Can you imagine how this relationship would have went if we shared a vision, but hadn't developed a plan to see it through? We would have surely fallen short of our goals. Soon after we learned the importance of both purpose and process, BVN began to develop a plan of action that facilitated measurable goals, timelines, and clear action steps to spark growth and accountability.

A Plan Is About Stewardship

We want to steward our personal and professional lives to make the biggest impact we possibly can. When we are good stewards of what has been entrusted in our care, more comes our way! So it's crucial that you are prepared for more. I have met so many business owners and leaders that want growth, but they're not ready for it. They often have a strong vision for growth and can get others excited about it. Sales may even begin to pick up. However, with no real plan in place to facilitate growth, they can't truly manage it.

When we live and breathe stewardship by developing a personal plan of action first, we position ourselves for manageable success. I always say that God will open the door, but what walks us through it is preparation. We want to be prepared for success and growth. Therefore, taking proactive steps in strategic development is the way to go. A personal plan of action prepares us for success in our personal vision.

My wife and I are committed to examining our personal finances together 2 times per year. Honestly, this used to be one of my least favorite things to do with Karen - a far cry from an exciting date night. Now, with a different perspective, it is something that I'm actually excited about. The results that come out of these pre-planned meetings are worth the effort.

After taking a closer look at what comes in and what goes out, we can create a plan that helps us stay within our means and work toward our dreams. Isn't it interesting that almost every time we follow this exercise, unexpected money comes in, interesting new business developments are ignited, and debts are looked upon more favorably? Suddenly, it becomes easy to look forward to financial meetings!

Practical Step: Plan Ahead

What does the plan for your life look like? Based on what came out of your dream session last chapter, let's take a look at the next 12 months and 2 solid steps to jumpstart your plan.

Create Your Vision Mantra

If you were to create an overarching mantra for your life for the next year, what would it say? This mantra will be the lens through which all things filter for the next 12 months. For example: "Work smarter, not harder!"

5 Positive Outcomes

What are 5 outcomes you'd like to see in the next 12 months?

These are goals that you have a high level of certainty about – not just a guess. Remember, it's all about perspective! State these outcomes in specific and positive terms. In a sense, they become positive declarations we live by throughout the year. 5 main areas of any well-balanced personal vision plan include: Spiritual, Family, Career, Mental, and Physical.

For example:

Family Outcome - My family and I will operate in greater unity this year.

Create Monthly Action Steps

Create a 3-month timeline. This means 1 action step each month for each of your 5 Outcomes. Identify someone who can hold you accountable. This will help you overcome blocks and reach your goals. Continue this every 3 months throughout the year.

For Example:

January: Go out as a family to the movies
February: Schedule a baby sitter for date night
March: Have a date night with Karen

PART III

The Big "Why" Behind
Your Business

CHAPTER 10
Your Business Vision Plan

Aʜ, ᴛʜᴇ ᴛɪᴍᴇ ʜᴀꜱ finally come to take a look at your business. This is the time of the Inside Out Leadership process that we finally look at the outside. Now you can take all your Inside Out Leadership inspiration and start viewing your business through this ultra-focused lens.

You are ready!

Whether you are a seasoned business owner or leader, aspiring entrepreneur, or someone who wants to take a creative idea and put some meat on its bones, this is for you. Also, some of you leadership veterans will see this process as a time of refreshment and refocus!

Did you know that your business is a person? It sounds funny, however, governments view businesses as legal entities, so why shouldn't you? As a matter of fact, as a business leader, you mentor this "person" that is your company. You spend a considerable amount of time coaching them and influencing them. Interesting, right? As you can probably see now, that's why it's so critical to work on yourself first.

The Business Vision Plan answers the foundational questions: Who?

What? Where? Why? Answering these questions for any business or business idea is paramount and needs to be revisited at least once per year. This is how you will define (or redefine) your business!

WHO Is Your Business?

Imagine you're on an elevator with a highly influential business investor who's looking to invest in a company in the next few days. You have 30 seconds. The investor turns to you and asks that pivotal question.

"Hey, what is it that you do?"

The very words that come out of your mouth may lead to the deal of your life. This next exercise will prepare you for that moment.

What descriptive words would you use to paint a vivid picture of your business and draw them in? I like to call these your "power words." Upon being spoken, these power words give a strong visual of **who** you are as a business.

As we learned in Chapter 6, if you want to know why you exist, you have to know who you are! Therefore, if you want to know why your business exists, you have to discover or rediscover **who** your business is. Sometimes it helps if we think about how we normally describe other people. We may describe a friend in such terms as: "She's **fun**, she **laughs** a lot, she's so **energetic**, she's a total **extrovert**." Another person's description might sound like, "Every time I'm around him, he just brings a sense of **peace** to the room and **helps quiet my soul**."

Have you ever described your business in similar terms? For instance, my global consultancy, Holman International, is a purpose-driven and passionate global leadership training organization. We partner with business owners and leaders who want to maximize their leadership ability.

What words would you use to describe your business, department, or idea that would tell this investor who your company is? The more refined you can make it, the better. With these words, you create interest that may lead to another conversation. We're essentially talking about the art of effective communication in networking.

As powerful as this is to do on your own, try going through this descriptive process on a consistent basis with team members and advisors. You'll become truly in sync with one another.

Here are a couple of other great examples of businesses answering their WHO:

1. **Yellow Leaf Hammocks:** In addition to sustainable social change, we believe passionately in **travel,** naps, good food, great **friends,** long talks, broadened horizons + a **spirit of adventure.**
2. **Eight Hour Day:** We're Eight Hour Day, a creative studio that loves to learn, collaborate, and create.

WHY Does Your Business Exist?

Once we know who we are as a business, we can better grasp our existence as a business. This is the **purpose** of your company. One practical way to discover or rediscover why your company exists is to identify some specific problems within your market that you solve. Also, take a closer look at what your ideal client needs and identify the gaps that you/your competitors are not filling.

For Holman International, we noticed some problems business owners and leaders were facing (mentioned in the introduction), and we wanted to do something about it! Here's what we found:

- According to a survey by Deloitte University Press, nearly 90% of workers interviewed admitted that they were not excited about their careers.

- According to a survey by Deloitte University Press, nearly 80% of business owners and leaders are not passionate and purpose-driven in the work they do.
- A Gallup poll estimated that the U.S. alone wastes $500 billion each year in lost productivity!

Based on this information and so much more, we have determined that our purpose at Holman International is to help leaders gain more purpose and passion through our exclusive Inside Out Leadership process. We do this through our speaking, training, and coaching.

Lastly, it's important to remember that the average customer longs for consistency when it comes to your WHY message. Whether it's digital media, hard-print material, the spoken word, or any other avenue of communication, customers are waiting to experience a consistent message every time you interact. The most successful organizations have a well-defined message and stay true to that message across the board. Here are some simple WHY statements from well-known organizations:

Boeing: To push the leading edge of aviation, taking on huge challenges and doing what others cannot do

Merck: To preserve and improve human life

Nike: To experience the emotion of competition, winning, and crushing competitors

Telecare: To help people with mental impairments realize their full potential

Teaching Co: To ignite in all people the passion for learning

Sony: To experience the sheer joy of advancing and applying technology for the benefit of the public

Becton-Dickinson: To help all people lead healthy lives

Walt Disney: To make people happy

WHERE Is Your Business Going?

Writing a good vision statement shouldn't be too difficult. As a matter of fact, it's the perfect opportunity to project a positive future state that energizes and inspires you moving forward. A simple and compelling vision will attract passionate team members who are willing to make the sacrifices necessary for the long haul. To be clear, this is not a feeling of obligation, rather, a feeling of being integral to something much larger than them.

Think about where your company would go in an ideal world. Where would you aspire to go if there were no barriers holding you back? Think far enough forward that you can separate yourself from the present. A time frame of about 10 years is sufficient.

Summarize your vision thoughts into a brief statement that reflects WHERE you're heading and the image you want to build along the way.

What does a positive end-state look like both internally and externally? What is the end destination of you living out your purpose? It may help to think about those within your organization and those that you impact outside of the organization. Keep in mind that you don't want to be too generic or too narrow-minded. If you are too general, you can water down your vision, and if you are too narrow, you can limit your vision. Find a good middle ground.

Language is important. It's powerful to begin a business vision statement with "We dream of…", "We see…", "Our vision is to be…", or "Our vision is to put into action…"

Remember what we discussed in Chapter 8 about the power of personal vision. Return to this take some of the practical things in your personal vision and apply them to your business. Remember:

1. Purpose is the foundation from which we dream!
2. A vision trip will provide clarity toward future opportunities
3. Engaging ALL of your senses will help bring your dreams into reality.

Here are a couple of familiar companies and their vision statements:

PepsiCo

"Our vision is put into action through programs and a focus on environmental stewardship, activities to benefit society, and a commitment to build shareholder value by making PepsiCo a truly sustainable company." (Quoted from Pepsi Co.)

Amazon

"Our vision is to be earth's most customer-centric company; to build a place where people can come to find and discover anything they might want to buy online." (Quoted from Amazon.com)

WHAT Matters To Your Business?

Core values steer your business toward the realization of its vision. Day in and day out, core values are extremely important to practice. Your business must stand firm in living out these values no matter what is going on. I like to think of these values as deep convictions of the heart that you will not waver from, and certainly not compromise. These values make up a core belief structure that helps you sift through decisions, both small and large.

"Are we going to partner with this person or not? Are we going to align ourselves with this organization or not? Do we get an investor or not?"

Knowing WHAT matters will guide you through these decisions.

Let's say you have to make a strategic hire. You have 2 very capable applicants, but 1 is more in alignment with your business values. Who will you hire? It's a no brainer! Many times I have hired or encouraged others to hire based on core value alignment rather than skill alone. Obviously, I think the best of both worlds is ideal, but if I had to choose, I'd choose value alignment over skill any day. I have seen so many businesses hire based on skills alone and little-to-no cultural fit. Often, it spells disaster. On the other hand, I've seen companies take someone with a strong value alignment and little experience and make them great! Core values are a huge part of the business culture, or the "DNA" of your business.

I believe that core values are not so much what you aspire to, but what you already live from day in and day out. Often, this is revealed in where you spend your time, how you spend your finances, and how you make decisions. I find that so many businesses aspire to have a certain set of core values because they feel pressured by the market, industry, and competitors. The problem is, if they don't already live from these convictions today, chances are, they are pushing for something that is not at their core. Now, I'm not against aspiring toward something. But I would much rather you aspire toward what is truly in your heart - something *you* value. You know by now that Inside Out Leadership is about discovering or rediscovering what is at your core and unearthing it, as opposed to striving toward what you are not.

When developing core values, choose a minimum of 3 and no more than 5. This is the optimal range. It keeps the business focused, and it's easy to live and breathe these values within your organization. Also, you'll want to know why each value is crucial to your business. Give 3 reasons why for each core value. By the end of answering the 3rd why, you will start getting to the root of why a specific value matters to you.

Lastly, WHAT does this specific core value mean to you and your business? If you take the value of excellence, for example, it may mean something different to your business than it does to another business. Define each core value during this process so that you, your team, and your entire organization can own these values.

Here are a couple of examples:

Wegman's Food Markets

Our "Who We Are" Values:

- Caring
- High Standards
- Making a Difference
- Respect
- Empowerment

Bright Horizons Family Solutions

Core Values Statement: The HEART Principles:

- Honesty
- Excellence
- Accountability
- Respect
- Teamwork

Now that you have a better understanding of who you are, it's time to do the same for your business!

1. WHO is this person?
2. WHY is this person here?
3. WHERE is this person going?
4. WHAT does this person value?

CONCLUSION

I AM CONVINCED THAT IF we want to close the gaping engagement gap in the modern workplace, it begins with *you*, the leader!

As we learned in Chapter 6, when leaders lead from the inside out, they draw from their personal purpose and inject that enthusiasm into their professional lives. Once their true purpose is clarified, they can unleash its power in all areas of life – including their careers. When living out this passionate and blended life, others can't help but join in!

Inside Out Leadership promotes the unique perspective that your life is a holistic wheel with many spokes, not separate boxes that you navigate between. I always like to say that you take yourself with you wherever you go, thus there is no real separation.

In developing and fostering this way of life and leadership, you will be a healthier and more vibrant spouse, friend, neighbor, parent, mentor, sibling, son/daughter, and of course, business leader! The healthier YOU are, the healthier your business will be. The more purpose-driven YOU are, the more purpose-driven your business will be. The more focused YOU are, the more focused your business will be.

Applying the Inside Out Leadership principles is a proven, practical, and highly reproducible value system on life and leadership that will help you *Lead the Way*. As a business owner and leader, I've been in your shoes. I *am* in your shoes, and I'm here to help you embody all that you are while removing any barriers that hold you back. I firmly believe that better people make better businesses, better businesses make better communities, and better communities make for a better world!

Lead the Way is all about giving you the much-needed time to reflect on the things that matter so that you can give those things to others. Because you matter. Your life matters. You are more important than your business.

So, where do you go from here?

It is important to know that you were never meant to go at this thing called life and leadership alone. There is a growing *Lead the Way* movement that is here for you! Our community is committed to making sure that you remain inspired, encouraged, and also have practical resources to help you on your Inside Out journey. In light of this, we have given you a special code below to join *Lead the Way*, our password-protected community at **www.leadthewaybook.com/ jointhemovement**

Sign in using this passcode: **LTW17RJH** (This passcode is only good for purchase of the book and will also give you **access to the Inside Out Leadership Check-Up!**)

LEARN MORE...

Robb Holman is an internationally recognized leadership keynote speaker and trainer who helps audiences connect with their unique life's purpose and find success in a way they never expected - from the inside out!

If you're interested in having Robb give a passionate keynote talk or experiential training workshop on *Lead the Way* or learn more about his Inside Out Leadership™ products and services, visit:

www.robbholman.com
To Interact with Robb, visit:
Twitter: www.twitter.com/robbholman
Facebook: www.facebook.com/robbholman1
LinkedIn: www.linkedin.com/in/robbholman
YouTube: www.youtube.com/c/robbholman

To Take The
Inside Out Leadership™ Check-Up *Visit:*
www.leadthewaybook.com/**jointhemovement**

Sign In

Using This Passcode.

LTW17RJH

This passcode is good for one person only.

🌐 **http://www.robbholman.com**

✉ **info@robbholman.com**